HOW
NOT
TO
Get
Promoted

HOW
NOT
TO
Get
Promoted

*Fix the self-sabotaging
behaviors holding you back*

Emily Kumler

HARPERCOLLINS
LEADERSHIP

AN IMPRINT OF HARPERCOLLINS

Published by HarperCollins Leadership, an imprint of HarperCollins Focus LLC.

Published in association with Kevin Anderson & Associates: https://www.ka-writing.com/.

Book design by Aubrey Khan, Neuwirth & Associates.

ISBN 978-1-4002-1856-1 (eBook)
ISBN 978-1-4002-1845-5 (HC)

Library of Congress Control Number: 2020936192

Printed in the United States of America
20 21 22 23 LSC 10 9 8 7 6 5 4 3 2 1

Contents

Section 1
Getting to Know Yourself

Section 2

Making an Impression

Section 3

Getting the Offer

A Special Dedication

This book is dedicated to my sister Kate. Her vivid, emotional, hilarious storytelling makes me smile years after the telling has ended. She is the star of the family who rarely gets the credit she deserves. As a sister, a mother, and a friend she has set a great example for me. And when it comes to getting promoted, she has encouraged and believed in me since my first business endeavor, selling hot chocolate in front of the town exchange. Thank you for a lifetime of support. I love you.

To Sandy, Marci, Carrie, and Natalie, thank you for holding space for me and keeping me grounded in all our worlds!

A special thank-you to Katy, Doug, Anne, Nicola, Jessie, Jessica, Payal, Lindsey, Jason, Kate TR, Harley, Ames, and big

Camilla. I am acutely aware that every time I have fallen, broken in two, and wanted to hide in a pit of doom, you've come into the darkness, found me, held my hand, and shared in my sorrow. Then you've carefully and gently encouraged me, reminding me to get back up, to keep trying, and to be true to my ideas. Risk-taking is less risky when you know you have an incredible crash pad. Failure doesn't feel so final when friends unrelentingly believe you'll find a way—maybe not the way you thought—but that you'll find a solution to the problem. I'm endlessly grateful for your love and encouragement. Without it, I would surely be a different person.

Thank you to Mom, Dad, Kate, Dave, Aden, Marge, George, Robin, Michael, Billy, and Greta for being my family.

To my children, who have taught me the value of time and the fleetingness of it. How we spend our time and with whom we spend it are by far the most important choices we make in life, a lesson you both have driven home for me. I will always want more time with you. Being your momma is my favorite job and my greatest honor. I love you.

And to Bobby, my great love, who constantly deals with my unsolicited advice. Your drive and intellect are unmatched. Your determination to find the truth, to question everything, to pursue the unpopular, inspires me every day. I'm deeply indebted that you're on this journey with me. Thank you for giving me the space and freedom to pursue what I believe matters. Your opinions are always the ones I value most. When we don't agree, I know it means I'm about to learn something important because your thoughtfulness is always revealing to me. And nothing is more validating than having your support and love. I'd be lost without it. Thank you for sharing this life with me. I love you.

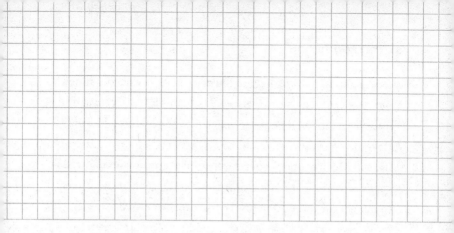

Introduction

Errare humanum est—to err is human.

When it comes to not getting promoted, you are likely the biggest obstacle in your way. Your ability to assess your own contributions, experience, readiness, and the assurance that you will succeed in the new position are all subjective. You may think you can check all those boxes, but if you're not evaluating yourself properly, you're in for a world of disappointment. Likewise, if you discount yourself too much, your lack of confidence might keep you in the same position longer than is warranted.

There are some basic facts about *not getting promoted* we should address up front. This book considers factors that are within your control. It is full of examples of how people have screwed up their chances at a promotion. Just like a fairy tale, the morals in these stories help to illustrate exactly what you should *not do*. My intention is that this book will be fun to read and informative for anyone interested in how to get ahead. However, it would be irresponsible not to address head-on how discrimination, which is out of your control, may impact your ability to get a promotion. The fact is: if you're a woman, you're more likely to not get the promotion just because you're a female.

This is one area where you have a profound, innate advantage—if we're looking at it in this backward way of trying not to get promoted. All you have to do to get passed over is be born into your body. If you're born a woman, congrats! Your male counterparts are much more likely to be picked for a promotion than you based exclusively on their sex!

According to the 2019 *Women in the Workplace* annual study conducted by McKinsey & Company and LeanIn.org, the problem of not promoting women starts at the manager level and women aren't able to make up that gap at later stages of their careers. The report finds: "Progress at the top is constrained by a broken rung. The biggest obstacle women face on the path to senior leadership is at the first step up to manager. For every 100 men promoted and hired to manager, only 72 women are promoted and hired. This broken rung results in more women getting stuck at the entry level and fewer women becoming managers. Not surprisingly, men end up holding 62 percent of manager-level positions, while women hold just 38 percent."[*]

And the report finds this issue is widely overlooked by hiring managers and human resource representatives. "More than half

---

[*] *Women in the Workplace, 2019,* McKinsey & Company. Accessed at https: //womenintheworkplace.com/.

of HR leaders and employees think their company will reach gender parity in leadership over the next 10 years. In reality, we are many decades away from reaching gender parity at the highest ranks—and may never reach it at all."

We find a similar hiring bias with most minority groups.

The research indicates that women are promoted less and paid less than men. But there are things you can do about it. I'd argue being aware and conscientious of this disadvantage is the first line of defense against it. And, for those who don't face this unfair disadvantage, you will have a role to play when you're promoted and afforded the opportunity to build your team; try to build one that includes lots of people who don't look like you. We all need to be aware of these prejudices and do our part to confront them and correct them. This book will *not* get into these innate reasons why you may not be promoted. Instead, it will look closely at actions within your control that will impact whether you get the big raise or jump a few rungs on the corporate ladder. It is important to distinguish between these two avenues of advice, both of which warrant more discussion and have direct bearing on who moves up and who doesn't.

> ∨   *This book will **not** get into these innate reasons why*
> ∨   *you may not be promoted. Instead, it will look closely*
> ∨   *at actions within your control that will impact*
> ∨   *whether you get the big raise or jump a few rungs on*
> ∨   *the corporate ladder. It is important to distinguish*
> ∨   *between these two avenues of advice, both of which*
> ∨   *warrant more discussion and have direct bearing on*
> ∨   *who moves up and who doesn't.*

My goal with this book is to help you think about how people sabotage or miss out on their promotions so you will be ready to seize yours when the time comes.

Now that we've addressed the discrimination-elephant in the room, we can get into non-innate examples of people messing up their chances at a promotion.

Anyone looking to get promoted needs to consider how they might screw it up, because all too often we get in our own way and flub opportunities that should have been ours. This book will help you see where people go wrong so you can get it right.

The stories included in this book are amalgamations of stories I've heard, reported on, or experienced firsthand. All accounts are fictionalized representations. Names and places have all been changed, details have been altered, but the lessons remain. My hope is that these stories will inspire an introspective look into how your actions and approach contribute—positively and negatively—to your successes. The more we learn about who we are, what motivates us, and what scares us, the more we can manifest the destiny we desire.

True intuitive expertise is learned from prolonged experience with good feedback on mistakes.   –Daniel Kahneman

HOW
NOT
TO
Get
Promoted

Getting to Know Yourself

Insecurities and Motivations Drive Actions

We swallow greedily any lie that flatters us,
but we sip only little by little at a truth we find bitter.
—Rameau's Nephew. *book by Denis Diderot, 1821*

We live in a reactionary time. With social media, twenty-four hour news, global trade and travel, our senses are exposed to much more than in our past. This constant bombardment of images, ideas, and opinions creates a state of compulsory responses. Rarely do we sit in stillness and open our senses to the calm and quiet of nothingness. Even the trends of mediation and mindfulness are clear indications of our desires to react to the state of reacting!

When you're working, you are also usually in a state of reacting. You are responding to the requests of your bosses, your clients, and so forth. And when you think you're ready for a promotion, that is often also a reactionary experience. You hear the job above you is being filled and you want it. A colleague suggests you apply for a higher position. Your partner says you deserve a raise. Or you think of a great idea for a new project that will elevate your position. But in all of these cases it is worth taking a beat to think about why you want what you want. Why is now the time to move up? Why is that specific position right for you? Where will that position lead you? Once you've done a deep dive into the whys, then you can start coming up with the *hows*. How are you going to get it? How will you transition your current workload? What can you bring to the new position? The answers to these questions will light your way, but you need to start with the basics, which means start with you.

Try to be aware of your reactions. Do you want the job because you think it's your turn and you don't want anyone else to have it? Do you want the new job exclusively for the title or the pay increase? Do you crave validation from your boss that you've been doing a good job? Whatever the motivation may be, recognizing it will help you keep it in check as you navigate the process of getting promoted—or losing out on a promotion.

Taking a hard look at what your insecurities are and what drives you will reveal a lot about what inner work you need to do. In the end, you do not want to pass up a promotion that would have been a great fit for your career path, nor do you want to rush into a position that will not fulfill you.

ONE

Don't Work on Your Insecurities, Instead Blame Everyone Around You

I t can't be your fault. They just don't like you. No one treats you with respect, so why should you respect them? Your ideas are never good enough. Someone else always gets the credit. Why work hard when no one notices? You're always blamed when *you* never make mistakes. Why is it always you who has to stay late? Why can't they see he messed it up? You didn't know. No one told you the right way to do it!

If any of those expressions sound familiar, you have some inner work to do. Whether you're a senior manager or an intern, just about every industry recognizes that working in a collaborative, helpful way is a winning strategy. Taking responsibility and contributing in a meaningful way will win managers' hearts and minds. Accepting feedback and working on weaknesses is never a bad idea. Yet many of us struggle with these powerful approaches.

- ∨ *Whether you're a senior manager or an intern, just*
- ∨ *about every industry recognizes that working in a*
- ∨ *collaborative, helpful way is a winning strategy.*
- ∨ *Taking responsibility and contributing in a*
- ∨ *meaningful way will win managers' hearts and minds.*
- ∨ *Accepting feedback and working on weaknesses is*
- ∨ *never a bad idea. Yet many of us struggle with these*
- ∨ *powerful approaches.*

Blaming others, not volunteering, complaining, and back-stabbing are great ways *not* to get a promotion. But, they are also easily accessible feelings in moments of perceived injustice. Bosses want to promote workers who have set good examples, not those whose ambitions and insecurities present a take-no-prisoners modus operandi. Yet, when we feel marginalized, ignored, or disrespected, our protective measures take over. We reject the unfair action and respond by upping the ante in our minds. The offender becomes an enemy. The hurtful words become a revenge-laden mantra replayed by our inner voices. Our narrative about the interaction, including the feedback, person, tone, implications, etc., becomes entrenched and soon we're convincing others of the wrongdoing. We are soon enough the ones misbehaving.

Very often our insecurities drive our bad behavior. It is essential to check in on your feelings of inadequacy; we all have them. Ask yourself: Are these feelings founded? Sometimes our insecurities point us toward areas we need to work on, skills begging to be developed and weaknesses that we have been hoping will just go away. In those cases, you have identified a terrific opportunity to grow; stop putting it off. Work on it, as those insecurities are not serving you well.

The other kinds of insecurities that can get us in trouble are the ones that bring up a displaced emotional response. If an interaction makes you feel sad, hopeless, angry, or vindictive, it is likely a response to something deep inside of you that's begging to be examined. Ask yourself why a certain encounter sent you into a pit of despair or a fit of fury. What was it about that comment that unraveled you? Spend some time with that feeling and see if you can figure out where it came from. Most of us have deep-rooted insecurities that can manifest in selfish behaviors. If you grew up in a household where you didn't feel valued for your intellect, or your sense of humor, or your opinions, or you were neglected, you may find that when coworkers—or others you're in relationships with—make a comment that taps into your sense of self-worth, you overreact. Try not to. Instead, take a hard look at when you were made to feel that way before. What was that like? Why is that moment still stuck inside your emotional body?

Then look back at the conflict with the coworker and try to play it out without the emotional response. Remember, we all bring our own personal history to every interaction and when things are stressful or loaded, we can easily make false assumptions about other people that actually come from interactions with other people. This can create confusion and conflict. Being self-aware will protect you from projecting old wounds onto new relationships. This is worth spending some time on.

Doing this kind of deep work to understand what negatively motivates you will help you interact with others in a more positive and productive way. People who haven't looked within to really understand their own insecurities and motivations often find themselves isolated, defensive, depressed, and deep in a self-absorbed spiral.

For example, whenever you pitch an idea, you hear feedback like: "Well, that's interesting, I've never thought of it like that before," or "You know, that's *actually* a really good idea." And the "I never thought of it like that before" is translated by your insecurities to sound more like: *They think I'm so dumb that they're surprised I thought of something they hadn't.* And "that's *actually* a really good idea" becomes an affirmation that they're surprised *you* suggested anything useful, because they all think you're a moron.

Stop right there. You're not a moron and you were likely hired to help them come up with ideas they couldn't develop on their own, so let's put those mean, imaginary voices to bed. They are not helping you. Where is all of that coming from? Why do you feel so insecure?

A more confident and centered person would hear those comments and interpret them as compliments. The "actually" would be confirmation that the boss was impressed and, while he could have phrased it better, it implies an emphasis on authenticity. He really, really thinks it's a great idea. Likewise, the "I've never thought of it like that before" is contextualizing the impact of your idea. The boss is saying you were able to think of something in a whole new way. For a seasoned person to see a problem or solution in a new context is about the best compliment you can get because it means he listened, he understood, and he learned from your idea. But the insecure, self-centered version of you didn't get any of that positive feedback because she was too busy assuming the worst and feeling upset.

Being sensitive and aware of what motivates you in positive and negative ways is essential to advancing in your career. We all have insecurities, but people who don't work to understand their own issues will often act in selfish and reactionary ways that ultimately hold them hostage in their relationships. Negative thinking can become a self-fulfilling prophecy, so be aware of how you're feeling and what inspires those buried beliefs to pop up. Be very mindful of your inner voice and old wounds. Spend some time working on them. Think of them as an image you've likely seen over and over throughout your life and realize they may not be helpful to you anymore. If you can detach from them, you can move forward and grow in a positive direction.

> ∨ *Being sensitive and aware of what motivates you in*
> ∨ *positive and negative ways is essential to advancing*
> ∨ *in your career. We all have insecurities, but people*
> ∨ *who don't work to understand their own issues will*
> ∨ *often act in selfish and reactionary ways that*
> ∨ *ultimately hold them hostage in their relationships.*

Doing this work will allow you to feel validated for your ideas, work, and relationships. It will also allow you to hear the real criticism in a healthier way. If you're feeling defensive, it is very hard to listen carefully. When someone gives you feedback, you want to hear it, so you can learn and grow from it. We have a hard time doing that when our guard is up.

Key Takeaways

Ways to Center Yourself

Identify your insecurities and you will become a stronger player.

- Don't just listen to respond, listen to hear.
  - If I asked you what the other person said, would you be able to quote them back to me?
  - If I asked you how the speaker felt when they were talking, would you be able to accurately characterize their feelings?
  - If I asked you what they meant, would they agree?
- Imagine you are the person you're interacting with—what do they feel?
  - If your answer is "angry," "frustrated," or "mad," then you must ask why. Once you get to why, you can ask them: "This is a frustrating/infuriating/ disappointing issue; how can I help to fix it?" Try to drive the emotion toward an action.
  - Verbally recognizing the emotion will allow the speaker to correct you if you've picked up on the wrong emotion: "No, I'm not angry, but it does make me worried . . ." which you can then deal with. "I don't want you to worry, so let me tell you how I'm going to handle it and you can tell me if my plan makes sense or if we should come up with a new strategy."

- Verbally recognizing the emotion will also allow you to address how it made you feel and then give the speaker a chance to respond.
- This may be a hard statement to make, but it will clear the air and move you to the next stage in the process: "It sounds like you're disappointed in my presentation and you wished I'd been more prepared."
- The response will either be a correction, "No, I'm not disappointed, I'm . . ." or it will be a relief that you've recognized their feelings.

- Try not to translate. Take people at their word. If someone isn't being literal, allow them to clarify.
- Write down a list of your insecurities before facing a tense discussion.
- Take your list of insecurities and try to assign them a person or situation from your past so you can free them from your future. They are not you; they are the earlier experience.
- Remember the best way to grow is to have people give you constructive criticism. Think of it as a gift rather than an insult.
- When someone ignites an emotionally charged feeling in you, try to release it; do not hold on to it. Take the value of the comment but leave the emotion behind. The emotion belongs to the giver, not the receiver.

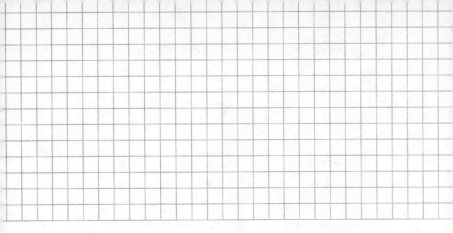

TWO

Be a Selfish Dick

By far the best way to be passed over for a promotion is to be a selfish dick. Making work, your relationships, the agreements, deals, and so forth all about *you* will surely keep you where you are, or maybe even get you canned. So, remember: Only you are important. Only your needs must be met. Only you are vulnerable. Only you deserve this. Only you are ever passed over. Only you.

If the goal of a promotion is to further the relationship with an employer, a project, etc., then it requires enough self-awareness to think about the others involved and the mission, which is larger than any one person. If you ignore all that, and instead focus on numero uno, you will not be promoted.

ᵛ *If the goal of a promotion is to further the*
ᵛ *relationship with an employer, a project, etc., then it*
ᵛ *requires enough self-awareness to think about the*
ᵛ *others involved and the mission, which is larger than*
ᵛ *any one person. If you ignore all that, and instead*
ᵛ *focus on numero uno, you will not be promoted.*

Consider these questions:

- Have I acquired the necessary skills to excel in the new position if I get it?
- What about the new job interests me most?
- Will I be good at the new gig?
- What will my new life be like with my new promotion?
- What will I do with all my new money?
- What will my friends think of my new title?
- I wonder how long it will take to get my new business cards?
- What promotion will I get after this one?

Now stop.

See what happened there? You went down the path of self-involved assumptions. Sure, the first few questions seemed reasonable. It is essential to evaluate whether you're a candidate for the promotion you're asking for, but it's a slippery slope to a fantasy world that's all about you. Stay on that track and you will stay in your mediocre job.

What if, instead, you ask yourself these questions:

- Who has been really successful in the role I'm hoping to be promoted into?
- What skills are required to be effective in that position?
- What skills/certifications/degrees/connections would be helpful in that position?
- What are the future-boss's visions for that role?
- Who can I talk to in order to learn more about the day-to-day responsibilities and the longer-term goals of that position?
- What are the experiences most successful candidates have had before they moved into that role?
- Who are the people that interact most with that role and how can I build relationships with them?

These questions get to the heart of the contribution you'll be making if you're promoted. They also scream that your intention is to drive impact for the company and team rather than for yourself, exclusively. The latter set of questions should be avoided if your goal is to not be promoted. Forget these contributions and go back to the fantasy of you on the yacht with the hot chicks and a massive raw bar. That's where your head needs to be if you want to be passed over.

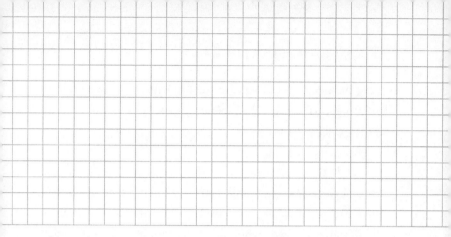

THREE

Group Projects Never Work
Go It Alone and Get All the Credit

Team projects can be a struggle. Most of us still have dreams—or nightmares, depending on the role you played—of a group project back in school that ended in disarray. Someone didn't do the work they were assigned. Someone else decided to take things in a new direction without consulting the team. Another member had a meltdown and went MIA. You, the hardworking group leader, were left standing before your classmates unsure of what to do.

The temptation to say, "Don't worry, I can take this one," may be strong, but resist. It is not only insulting to your colleagues, it also shows poor leadership skills to just take on the project and leave the others out. They also want to shine, so find a way to work together and you'll get points for a project well done *and* for the collaboration.

THE CLIENT WAS an upscale ice cream company out of Maine. They'd cornered the market in the late '80s and '90s using branding that linked them to popular music groups and an attitude that said, "Your parents like Häagen-Dazs, but you're cooler than that. You like Max & Steve's."

But now they were struggling to differentiate themselves. The college crowd was becoming more health conscious and their market hold was melting away.

When The Heather Blumenthal Agency was hired, they were clearly told: "Your job is to come up with a strategic plan that results in every college kid in America taking selfies with our top flavors." There weren't any limitations; the marketing experts could come up with new flavors, new ice cream innovations, new slogans. The sky was the limit if it would accomplish the goal.

Heather, the founder of the consulting firm bearing her name, loved projects like this. It was what had made her, and her agency, so well known. With hundreds of clients she could no longer be in the trenches with the teams, but she still loved the process. "When we take on big challenges, we see big results and our best employees rise to the top and I get to see who my next leaders will be. I just love everything about it."

She decided to make spots on this dream team a competition. Individual employees would pitch a panel on their ideas and then the executives would pick ten people to collaborate and work on the final pitch for the ice cream client.

Some of the ideas were fabulous. The executive team picked the best innovation idea, the best new slogan, the best celebrity partner pitch, and so forth, hoping together these players would present the ultimate pitch. Heather was optimistic the ten they'd selected would blow this up.

It was like being in a startup; designing everything from scratch and the thrill of not knowing how it would all play out was all the motivation they needed. At the very first meeting, everyone was excited to hear their teammates' ideas—collaboration was king. But by the midway point, things were falling apart.

Jack, who came up with the idea to put vending machines in all the biggest dorms next to the soda machines, was wallowing in deep-freezer tech, learning how cold machines needed to be, how long the ice cream could last, what contingency plans needed to be in place if the power went out and the product melted. He had essentially gone off on his own to make sure the vending ice cream concept was viable. It was his idea and the group was behind it, but they also realized that alone it might not be enough; they needed to offer the client more.

Julie was a rising star. She had come up with an idea for a major minivan account that had blown everyone away and put the firm on the top of most major automakers' lists of firms to work with. She had pitched the family automakers on turndown trays, just like in airplanes: the back of the driver's and passengers' seats had foldout tables for eating or drawing or whatever. She had also added cooler functions to the center consoles, which was a massive hit for all moms and dads desperate for some cold soda while carting kids around on hot summer days. For those two ideas she was basically the badass of the group. She'd signed off on Jack's idea for the vending machines, which pushed the rest of the group to follow suit. With this project, Julie was focused on the image of the company.

"They made their name by distancing themselves from the fancier brands, presenting instead as young, hip, even a bit scrappy—all while charging the same prices," Julie told the group after doing her own market research. "But now, those kids who were their best customers are grown-ups, so that distinction doesn't really work. I mean, most kids today know the brand as their parents' favorite ice cream, so the idea that we're identifying through generational separation or rejection won't work. We need something totally new."

"How about playing off their tradition of collaboration with music groups?" said Beth. "They had a lot of success with Metallica Mint and GnR'—Gummies n' Reece's. What if we did Bruno Mars Bars or Ariana Gramcrackers?"

Everyone smiled except Julie.

"Yeah, that feels old," Julie said. "They want new. I'm sure they could come up with clever, funny names for flavors. I think we can do better than that."

And just like that, Julie had separated herself from the group. She'd usurped veto power over other people's ideas. No one gave it to her, but she'd taken it, no permission needed.

"Well, I liked it," Jamison said, pushing back on the new authority. "I think the idea of sticking with some of their earlier themes would offer some consistency, allowing new, younger consumers to latch on while also invigorate the older demo— their die-hard fans. Why not work on both new and reinvigorating the old?"

Julie saw this pushback as a test and thought, if she relented, her power would be sucked back into the group. *This wasn't what they hired us to do*, she thought. *I want to shine on this project. Heather is watching closely and if I get two back-to-back wins, I'm sure she'll promote me.* Julie's inner voice was taking over. "Because, it's misguided. They don't want us to reinvent their broken wheel, they want us to create a new one."

At that moment, the energy shifted. Somehow it felt to Julie like it was her against the team. She knew the feeling well. Why wasn't anyone else like her? Why was everyone so stuck, unable to think outside the box? This project had so much potential, so much freedom, and she was going to get pigeonholed with these losers. It was so frustrating, especially coming off the double win with the minivan—she couldn't let their lack of imagination destroy her career momentum. The big promotion was one big win away and she wasn't going to let them take it from her.

If we pause the story for a minute here, we can all see how Julie is setting herself up for sabotage. But there is a subtlety I think we all fall prey to in group dynamics. There are naturally people who are louder, more outwardly confident, and they will dominate the conversation. Those who are quieter may have better ideas, but may not get to express them, or when they do, their ideas may be shot down quickly. After an interaction like this one between Julie, Beth, and Jamison, a more reserved person would likely remain quiet and that might prevent the group from advancing. Everyone watches power-play dynamics and takes different things from the interactions, most of which will stymie creative thinking and group cohesion. Teams are only as good as the worst listener on them. Meaning, if there are people who dominate and do not listen, then the whole team will suffer. Collaboration is about listening. Julie has forgotten that.

As the process moved along, the sides became more defined. Those in Julie's camp were dialed in on her big idea: keto ice cream. It wouldn't have carbs and it would be loaded with fat and keto fanatics could eat it as a meal. The slogan was: "Your parents ate ice cream for dessert and got fat. You eat it for dinner and stay fit." Julie was running the whole thing, from finding ingredients that would work to getting the right experts to weigh in on how ice cream could be healthy for dinner. But she only had one other teammate pitching in because now she was polarizing, and the others didn't want to buy in on her Julie-rule. She used this to fuel her ambition. *They'd be sorry when her idea won the day,* she thought.

   ∨ *Teams are only as good as the worst listener on*
   ∨ *them. Meaning, if there are people who dominate*
   ∨ *and do not listen, then the whole team will suffer.*
   ∨ *Collaboration is about listening.*

The other group was revamping old campaigns, enlisting big-name musicians to lend their support and likeness. Their ideas weren't entirely original, like Jack's or Julie's, but they were an evolution of the brand's core strategy. The new look was fresh, but not revolutionary. The six teammates had divided up the duties and together they were confident their ideas were executable tomorrow. They felt good about how the pitch stayed within the tradition of the brand *and* would open the doors to the younger market.

Jack had become an expert in vending machines and was sure his concept would work. In fact, he wondered if he should patent it, but there was no time for that; the presentation was rapidly approaching.

When the big day arrived, the team assembled in a small conference room with not enough chairs for everyone around the oval pine table. It felt like every part of this project was an alpha dog contest—who would get a chair, who would be listened to, whose idea would move up the ranks, who would get the credit ... None of this felt like collaboration. It was more like Survivor Island.

"Well, I, for one, am very proud of the work we've done," Julie announced, clearly speaking to her helper, Brit, rather than the group at large. "I think Jack's vending machine is brilliant, I think the client is going to love our new product line, and of course they may also like the traditional concept."

It was the best she could muster: a compliment with a lot of baggage. Julie locked eyes with Brit, who was standing behind her and dutifully nodding in affirmation. Brit had done a lot of work for Julie on this project and hadn't tried to claim a seat.

Jack was proud of his team's work, but he didn't feel the need to get into the pissing contest. He stayed seated while Beth took the floor. "Right, sure, Julie. I would just like to say that I think we've come up with some great ideas and we're going to kill it in there! Go team!"

Half the table smiled at Beth's cheerleader performance; the other half looked like they were trying to avoid eye rolls. They all knew they needed to go in as a team, to at least appear connected to one another. Heather had been talking up the presentation around the office for months and was going to be sitting with the clients during the presentation.

Julie gave the overview, Beth introduced the team members, and then the three ideas were presented. It seemed like the client liked all of the ideas as they were smiling and nodding. The critique was next.

"I love the vending machine idea," Camilla, the CEO of the ice cream company, started. "It's novel, it's innovative, it gets at our demo where our demo lives, all wonderful. I'm onboard. My mind is racing at the possibilities here. I mean why wouldn't we put these on playgrounds, in hospitals, everywhere? Anywhere people are buying soda they could be buying ice cream! Love! Love! Love!"

"Thank you, I'm thrilled you like it," Jack said, standing in the front of the room.

"Oh, and, best of all, I love that you fitted it with our individual serving containers. I can't tell you how often people pitch ideas that sound cool, but in practice turn into a nightmare for our manufacturing division. Engineers like problem solving, sure, but they don't always like to come up with a whole new design to fit someone else's ideas, especially when we have a design that works already. One of the best parts of this idea is that it's simple, a plug and play with a product we already make. This makes me think it's implementable tomorrow, and that's everything in our business. Simple, implementable quickly and easily, and cost efficient. Bravo! This is a big win!

"Let's turn to the two other campaigns for a moment," Camilla continued. "I'm a little confused why these feel so different. Your pitch should have used the vending machines as the core and then built out from there, at least that's how I'd see it. So, tell me, how did you come up with the ideas for both a new product line and for a revamping of our current line? These don't seem to work harmoniously."

Camilla had hit the nail on the head. They were the products of disharmony. But Julie thought she could talk her way through it. Now it wasn't about her idea or Beth's; they needed a shared narrative or else this pitch would fall flat.

"I can see why you'd think that," Julie began. "I too had questions about revamping the musical link, but we thought if we offered something new to the younger demo with the new top stars, it might bring back the older customers and excite the younger crowd, and . . ."

"I think what Julie means," Beth interjected—it was her research after all . . . "is that our in-depth demo research showed there was still a strong appeal, as you all had found in the '90s, to link your products, by name, with celebrities. We loved how you capitalized on musicians, which provides sponsorship opportunities and lots of cross-promotion that wouldn't be possible with, say, a movie star, but we found that kids still love ice cream and, especially in college, offering a fun snack for late-night munching would do well if linked with their favorite singer. I thought we could feature these new flavors in the college vending machines, maybe even tie it together with concerts playing on campus. There are loads of opportunities to get kids posting about their fave new flave! It's going to be awesome."

"And I love your energy around it," Camilla said. "We also believe in staying true to our core brand, which this campaign certainly does. I can imagine parents dropping their kids off at college, we could have a welcome tent handing out the new flavors, and a funny conversation taking place where the dad is joking about his old-timer favorites. Anytime we can help create those sentimental moments, I'm all in. But I'm still confused: Are these flavors going to be keto? How many college kids are keto? That seems like a completely separate pitch, no? Tell me how these all go together?"

All eyes turned to Julie. "Great question," she said, clearly stalling. "I think keeping up with the times requires more than just mixing a new artist with yet another variation of cookie dough ice cream. . . ."

"So you don't think the new flavors will be a success?" Camilla interrupted.

"No, I didn't say that, I think they may be, but I think what is missing in the ice cream market right now are products that help people stay on their diets. We have sugar added to our deli meats, and the public is becoming more educated on the deleterious effects of sugar and wanting, searching, for products that offer a healthier alternative. And, it turns out, ice cream could qualify. As I explained in the presentation, nutritionists and experts we spoke with told us that, because ice cream is mostly dairy, it has the potential to be the perfect keto food. The diet requires a high fat intake, which can be hard for people to get in our low-fat culture. But if we made a heavy-cream, no-sugar flavor, we'd have a killer keto product that everyone would love."

"I'm sure you know that the second ingredient in ice cream is sugar, right?" Camilla said with a smile, clearly trying to lighten the mood but making a point.

"Yes, of course, but there are new substitutes coming on the market every day. This is an incredible opportunity, a way of re-framing a dessert from being a treat on special occasions to an everyday, healthy thing."

"I got it, but to be fair, it's not really in line with the other two pitches. Or is it? I'm still confused," Camilla posed.

"Maybe you could name a keto flavor after a musician and put it in the vending machine? I don't see why not." Julie was feeling backed into a corner and was thinking on the fly. It wasn't a bad idea, but it hadn't been thought out because she hadn't collaborated with the other teams.

"Well, that's interesting. Why wasn't that in the presentation? Maybe that would have been the glue to hold this all together. Do the keto products require the same temp control? Will they fit in the same packaging? Are they all compatible with the vending machines?"

It was a great question, but no one had discussed it. And Julie, now on the spot, didn't know any of the vending machine stats or functionality requirements. It might be possible that, with all that fat mixed with the sugar substitute, it would require a different type of package. She just didn't know. So, she said just that: "I'm not sure, we didn't look into that."

"Okay, well thank you all very much," Camilla said, concluding the pitch meeting.

Later, Heather took Julie aside. "You all did a lot of work, it was exciting to watch, but I wonder what happened behind the scenes," Heather said. "You're usually such a great galvanizer, bringing everyone together and pushing the needle. This felt a little off for you."

"It was hard. I didn't love the revisiting of the old musical theme. I mean, that's kind of like swimming in someone else's pool when you have the chance to design your own, you know? I wasn't on board, and I thought the keto idea was a slam dunk. Jack was off being Jack, so he didn't really need any help. And so, we kind of all did our thing separately."

"Right, and that was the problem," Heather said. "Jack didn't need your help, but you all would have benefited from being a part of his process—it was far and away the best and safest idea out of the group. Didn't you see that?"

"Yeah, it was brilliant, but he didn't need anything, and you know, I wanted to contribute, I wanted to have my own idea come to fruition, like the minivan account. That was amazing."

"You occasionally have the best idea, but most of the time when you're working in a top talent place like this, you won't. You need to be cool with that. We have to collaborate because of that. Sometimes the best strategy is recognizing when someone else has a better idea and getting on board. That clearly didn't happen here. And frankly, sticking with a client's core values may not be as sexy as coming up with a whole new product, but let me tell you from my experience, companies have core values for a reason. They love them, they are everything, so you need to think long and hard before telling a CEO her values and that their key ingredients need an overhaul. Taking sugar out of ice cream is like taking Santa out of Christmas! Sure it may be what the market wants, but you need to explain that so clearly and rationally that even Mrs. Claus would be on board. That didn't happen. It was all too much, way too much, to have three new concepts that weren't seamlessly tied together. I know you're hungry and you'll move up, I'm sure, but you need to work on your leadership skills, your listening skills, before that will happen. Remember, it's not always about *you* having the idea, it's about helping the best idea advance that matters most. If you'd come up with a new flavor that was keto and was available in the vending machines, this would have been seamless, but that would have required listening and working together, which clearly didn't happen here."

Key Takeaways

Collaboration is all about listening carefully

- **Ask the right questions.** Saying "what do you think?" is helpful, but saying "how can we improve on this idea?" will generate better answers because the implication is that you're not wedded to the idea and if someone suggests something else, you're not going to be upset about it. Always try to frame your questions in a way that generates more ideas rather than closing the conversation off.

- **Create an environment where sharing is a part of everyone's process.** Start each meeting by having everyone introduce themselves and say what part of the process they're focusing on. This provides data and updates and also gives everyone at the table a voice and permission to speak.

- **When someone expresses an idea or suggestion that changes the course of the plan, explore it.** You do not have to commit to it, but asking why he thinks it's an important move or what about the current plan he thinks is broken will reveal something useful.

- **Gather as much data from the group as you can.** This starts with the brainstorming sessions in the beginning, but it should continue throughout the process. Often plans change, designs fail, new information comes to light, and the best groups are flexible and open to that process, but if you're not listening you will miss out on the opportunities to refine and grow.

Establish a list of behaviors to follow at each group meeting

- **If this group had started their first meeting by creating expectations, they would have avoided many of these pitfalls.**
- **Write out, for all to see, the agreed-upon process for how the group is going to share ideas and critiques.** Include how decisions will be made and how work will be delegated. It's not a bad idea to have one person be the overseer who manages these internal-group tasks.
- **Remember, getting promoted often rests on the individual's ability to lead, to bring others together, and to produce.** All the behaviors you set at the beginning of a group meeting will help position the team to excel, and each of its members will be more qualified for that promotion.

Set personal goals that are not tied to personal outcomes

- **Julie missed an opportunity in this case because she was determined to shine as an individual rather than as a group leader.**

- **If she'd chosen one of these goals, she would have been better off:**
  - Get to know everyone's strengths and weaknesses on my team.
  - Find areas to help support others with their processes.
  - Add value by connecting my pitch to others to create a cohesive pitch.
  - This is a talented team, but what's lacking is leadership. If I can help others connect and feel supported, the whole team will advance.
  - Helping others with their ideas will teach me valuable skills and insights into the areas they know more about than I do. Through this collaboration, I will acquire new skills by assisting my teammates.
- **In general, you want to set achievable goals,** and the goals that drive impact are always focused around where and how you can help drive impact, rather than where you can shine individually.

REMEMBER, WHEN YOU bring people together, you are viewed as a leader. When you isolate yourself, you are more likely to be left out of a winning strategy that could have led to a promotion.

FOUR

Tell Yourself You're Not Good Enough and Talk Yourself Out of the Promotion

As much as the egotistical employee destroys his chances at a promotion, so too does the worker who constantly doubts herself. If you're working hard, getting along with co-workers, meeting your goals, and exceeding expectations, you are probably ready for a promotion. But if you don't believe in yourself, that promotion may not manifest.

- ∨ *If you're working hard, getting along with coworkers,*
- ∨ *meeting your goals, and exceeding expectations, you*
- ∨ *are probably ready for a promotion. But if you don't*
- ∨ *believe in yourself, that promotion may not manifest.*

When Sydney developed the winning strategy that cata-pulted her client, a gymnastics apparel company, from a no-name to a household brand, she knew she'd done a good job. But was it good enough? Was it her best work? No. After all, the client was fairly small, though growing more rapidly now thanks to her, but she knew the bigger clients brought in more money and that was where her boss was focused, as she should be, Sydney thought. She wondered who in the firm knew that she'd created the two viral social media campaigns that gold medalists were now sharing and commenting on. That was all cool, but maybe it was just luck. She didn't see her boss making a fuss about it, so she wasn't about to bring it up. It obviously took a lot more than a few successful campaigns to move up the ladder. She understood. When the time was right, surely someone would let her know.

The only thing Sydney hated more than self-promotion was feeling like she'd let someone down. Many described her as shy, which she didn't really like, but she recognized why they thought that label fit. She personally preferred reserved or thoughtful, but she kept that opinion to herself. She'd never felt the need to add to conversations just for the sake of hearing her own voice, which she felt was an epidemic around the of-fice. But she did have opinions and hated when people inferred she didn't.

Now in her third year at Bramberg PR, she'd started to notice that the more boisterous coworkers were moving up while she remained in the same junior position. It didn't seem fair, but it was also hard to imagine herself in a corner office. *Maybe this was just how the world worked*, she thought.

Wouldn't her boss let her know when she was ready for a promotion? Does getting a promotion by default require self-absorbed proclamations of successes? She hated all of that, so she did her work and hoped someone would notice.

But, when no one did, she started telling herself that ipso facto meant she was actually no good. *Everyone else seems to be able to do these things so easily, without any stress, maybe that's why I'm not promoted, maybe I'm just not good at this*, she thought when her head hit the pillow at night.

As time went on, Sydney had concocted a narrative that went like this: "Sure I'm reliable, honest, and I work hard, but I'll never be a star. I am good at some things, but others take me longer than my coworkers. I am too quiet to be a boss and too reserved to demand more. I am who I am, and I won't be able to change, so I'd better get used to the junior-level job because it's all I'll ever have."

Depressed was an understatement for how she started to feel. On the heels of the big social media win, she should have been flying high; instead, she was in a pit of despair. If only she could be more like Arlo—he was so confident, nothing ever got to him.

Sydney stayed in her position much longer than she probably should have, because, even though she thought her feelings were internal, externally she disparaged her own work and it left others conflicted. "Why is Sydney always so down on herself? It's exhausting to constantly pump her up." Or, "Sydney seems to think she messed up. I thought it was great, but maybe I don't know the whole story." Or, "Sydney's nice. I didn't know she worked on that . . ." Her negative narrative became a self-fulfilling prophecy.

"Hey, Syd," Thomas said. "Great job with the gymnasts. You'll have to show me how you do that someday."

"Aw, thanks," Sydney replied. "I didn't really do much. I guess they just liked the post. Lucky really. Not sure how to teach luck, but happy to try."

"Dude, you did it twice, that wasn't luck," Thomas said.

"Yeah, thanks, who knows if I'll ever be able to do it again, ya know? But, yeah thanks."

Thomas left the conversation wondering if Sydney was being falsely modest or if she really didn't know how she did it. It didn't occur to him that her internal voice was telling her she was an idiot and would never be able to replicate the experience, so she shouldn't go around taking credit for it.

The voices in our heads are powerful. Listen to yours. If you're telling yourself you're no good, it will seep out into the ether and others will pick up on it. Try to recognize your work and your impact and feel proud, embrace your wins. You do not need to go around bragging, but you can't expect others to get behind you if you're not behind yourself. If you're lucky, your mom may tell you she believes in you when you're down and out, but don't expect a boss to constantly praise you and lift you up for doing a good job—that's what you were hired to do.

> ⌄ *The voices in our heads are powerful. Listen to yours.*
> ⌄ *If you're telling yourself you're no good, it will seep*
> ⌄ *out into the ether and others will pick up on it. Try to*
> ⌄ *recognize your work and your impact and feel proud,*
> ⌄ *embrace your wins.*

Most bosses, especially in highly competitive environments, are not great at validation. They may feel happy, maybe even proud, of your work, but they also specifically hired you because they wanted you to perform at a high level. You don't always get a gold star for doing a good job. Now, we could write another book on how bosses would get more out of their employees if they learned the basics of positive reinforcement, but we're considering who gets promoted and who doesn't. The hard truth is, confident people are more likely to appear capable and are therefore more likely to get a promotion. But, that doesn't mean there isn't room for the more reserved to find their stride.

> ⌄ *The whole "fake it till you make it" theory may work*
> ⌄ *for a big presentation, or a specific meeting, but it's*
> ⌄ *not a lifelong solution for someone who is more on*
> ⌄ *the quiet end of the spectrum. I'm a big believer that*
> ⌄ *you have to be true to you. Your best self will always*
> ⌄ *be your truest self.*

A lot of people will tell you to try to act like someone you admire. Pretend to be someone confident, and before you know it, you too will feel confident. I don't buy that. I think that's more likely to send you into the deep dark world of imposter syndrome than awaken some charismatic, confident person inside you who's been asleep at the wheel. The whole "fake it till you make it" theory may work for a big presentation, or a specific meeting, but it's not a lifelong solution for someone who is more on the quiet end of the spectrum. I'm a big believer that you have to be true to you. Your best self will always be your truest self. So, find her, hug her, and tell her to be brave and proud of her hard work. If your inner voice is talking shit about you, tell him to shut up. It's not helpful.

Make a list of the things the inner voice is saying and next to each one write an action that counterbalances the negatives.

Inner Voice	Action
You're too quiet	Speak up three times in your next meeting
No one likes you	Smile at four people in the hall and see who smiles back
Your work takes you longer	Ask a colleague how long it takes them to do a specific task and what their process is so you can improve yours, or accept that yours takes longer and that's okay because in the end the quality is what matters
People think you're dumb	Think of three research-based, relevant points to share with coworkers in a meeting

The best teams are made up of diverse voices and some of those voices are quiet. Being reserved is a gift if it means you're observing, taking in data, and are able to offer your insightful analysis. But the catch is, you must find your way to contribute. Without your contribution, you are more likely to be ignored or sidelined. Get to know the ways you prefer to communicate and use them to your advantage.

> ⌄ *The best teams are made up of diverse voices and*
> ⌄ *some of those voices are quiet. Being reserved is a*
> ⌄ *gift if it means you're observing, taking in data, and*
> ⌄ *are able to offer your insightful analysis. But the*
> ⌄ *catch is, you must find your way to contribute.*

If everyone is talking over one another in the conference room, find a way to express yourself without engaging in that kind of communication where you know you won't excel. Make a presentation, a visual aid, draft a memo or an email.

When you start in a new position, tell your boss how you feel you communicate best. She will appreciate this. Something like: "I'd also like to talk a bit about my process and communication strategy. I'm often told I'm shy. I don't think that's entirely accurate, but I understand why people say that. I don't have a domineering voice or personality. I've found I contribute best when I write out my ideas. For example, if you want me to pitch you on a social strategy, I will give you my best work by preparing something and creating a few examples to show you. I'm always happy to discuss your ideas, but I wanted to let you know I am often not as verbal as others tend to be. I want to contribute and do the best work possible, but I may approach it a little differently, which I hope you'll come to see works out well."

Setting the stage and the expectations of how you communicate accomplishes two goals: it shows your boss you know yourself and that you are taking the initiative to do the job in a way that will maximize your impact. Once you've established this dynamic, you may also find you feel more comfortable expressing yourself. You will have created an environment through those expectations that will allow you to thrive, rather than feeling like you're not enough when you're forced to play in someone else's sandbox. Create your own sandbox and you'll accomplish more and feel better about it.

Most bosses don't care if you're loud or you're quiet as long as you're getting the work done. Knowing that someone is their best when they work a certain way allows your boss to be a better boss to you, which in turn makes for a stronger team.

Many times, the things we feel insecure about are actually integral to our gifts. Don't waste your talent because it doesn't look like everyone else's; harness it by creating the right conditions for you to thrive.

Making
an Impression

Thinking is difficult, that's why most people judge. —Carl Jung

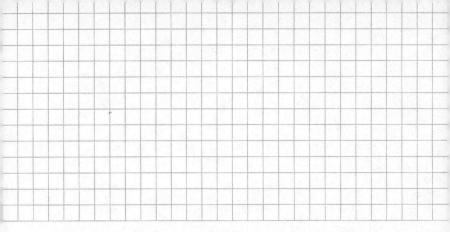

FIVE

Demand Attention

Don't Let Hierarchy Get in Your Way

It is dangerous to be right in matters
where established men are wrong. —Voltaire

Max ran a massive call center. Calls came in from people who had either just been offered a retirement savings account through their employer or clients who had questions about their retirement accounts. His firm managed millions of 401(k)s, IRAs, and pension accounts and the call center was ground zero for onboarding and troubleshooting.

Eighty rows of call banks forty-people deep filled a room the size of three Olympic pools. Max paced the lanes, like a swim coach observing his fish in the water. Eavesdropping and lightening the mood as he moved, Max knew all 1,600 representatives by name. He had twenty "hall monitors," as they were known, who helped him manage the floor, and each row had a captain. Max joked that his floor was like a tightly run aircraft carrier. Everyone had their place, their job, and most of the time things ran smoothly.

It could be a grueling job. New clients were happy, excited to be in a position to be offered retirement, and, in most cases, just needed to go through the administrative process of enrolling. But, more commonly, callers were frustrated or downright pissed off. If you've set aside money from your paycheck each week and you think it's not adding up fast enough, you feel entitled to answers. But those answers require a lesson in how the stock market goes up and down over time, not something all call center reps can handle. Worse still were the callers who realized the money they'd "saved" wasn't actually available to them. All too often clients would call up furious that they couldn't access their money without facing heavy taxes and fines for prematurely removing the funds. Those were the worst calls to get. Max wished the human resource representative responsible for onboarding clients did a better job explaining these restrictions, so his team didn't have to bear the brunt of the bad news.

You didn't know which type of caller you'd get until you accepted the call. There were some who believed it would be better to sort the calls by type and have dedicated specialists handle those calls, but Max believed the element of surprise that brings sweet anticipation to each call is what made the job exciting for most people. If you only had angry calls, you'd probably have higher turnover, whereas the suspense of picking up the call and not knowing what you were getting was reported by many to be the best part of the gig.

The primary reason people thrived in the position was the upward mobility awarded to those who handled themselves well. The pool, as it was known, was a breeding ground for the more senior sales positions. Learning the intricate details of all the products, all their corresponding restrictions, and how they performed over time was by far the best training program the firm had. Dealing with angry customers in a constructive way gave any sales rep the advantage of knowing what might go wrong and preempting the client's needs. Someone who came from outside the firm into a management role wouldn't have had this experience and would therefore be at a disadvantage. So, the pool was where most people started and the place where the best sales reps got their schooling.

Max loved his job. He had been offered promotions, but they would have all led to a four-walled office where he'd have been a fish out of water. This was his thing, he was good at it, and he liked bringing the new school of swimmers up to speed and into the ranks of management. He was like a talent scout, always assessing who was ready for the big leagues.

While everyone worked on their own, the pool was all about camaraderie. The row captains helped newbies, the newbies listened in on more seasoned teammates' calls, and they all cheered one another on.

The floor had unofficial ways of communicating. Headsets were wireless, so reps could stand, even walk around, though no one wanted to stray too far from the computer with the client's profile. It was nice not to be strapped to the desk, and the freedom allowed for nonverbal communication.

Ben's hand shot up from the middle of row sixteen. This signaled Jessica, the row captain, that Ben had a difficult client on the line. Jessica then hopped on Ben's call, listening to see how it was going.

The row captain would stand up if the caller was really out of line and the rep seemed to be handling it well. That would call over the hall monitor who would weigh in. If the hall monitor agreed this was an especially nasty or difficult call, she would signal to Max who would make his way over. When this happened, those who weren't on calls ignored their ringing lines. Those who were on a call hurried off. This happened a couple of times a day and it was another moment of anticipation built into the otherwise monotonous day.

Max had instituted this policy as a way of helping morale. When he started, he noticed employees crying. They were taking these calls personally. He'd tried reminding them that the callers didn't really know them; no one should tell you you're an idiot, or worse. But what really improved the morale on the floor was uniting everyone against the bad callers. Max would throw the worst of the worst on the PA system, allowing all 1,600 employees to hear the asshole. This removed the sting felt by the individual alone on the phone with the angry client and encouraged the team to help, to root for the call rep, and offer suggestions. It also offered a valuable teaching opportunity for the entire pool. Listening and watching someone defuse a bomb is perhaps the best way for others to learn.

And, it did something else: it made the call reps celebrities. In a sea of phone banks stocked with ambitious twentysomethings, the best way to distinguish yourself was to get a terrible call, get put on the megaphone, and handle it like a seasoned hostage negotiator. Suddenly, you'd go from being mostly unknown to being complimented at lunch, in the parking lot, and before you knew it, you'd have a nickname—usually something derogatory the caller had come up with—like Nuts for Brains, Tard Spawn, or Waste of Sperm, which would be turned into an acronym to avoid offending unknowing bystanders. This was when you'd made it.

A former rep had started tracking those with client-initiated nicknames and how quickly a promotion followed. It wasn't an exact science, but it was clear there was a connection between the two events.

Despite the clear harassment, everyone wanted to be on the loudspeaker showing their mad skills, but there were steps in the process. The last thing you wanted was to be on that speaker and screw it up. But Max had some safety precautions in place to avoid a nuclear meltdown under the pressure of having 1,600 ears tuned into your call.

When Max decided to put a call through to the PA system, he'd bring the rep over to the Shark Tank, as it was known. In the back-right corner of the pool, there was an alcove with two walls made up of dry erase boards. If you were the rep on the call, you'd stand in the middle. Reps from the floor would line up with suggestions, data, pieces of advice, or even phrases to use to help you through. As they listened, they contributed. You scanned the boards and erased ideas you didn't want to use, circled ones you liked. This made the call even more exciting, even more of a team process.

Ben had only been working at the firm for almost a year. He was smart and determined to move up the ranks. He showed up early and stayed late. Whenever there was an opportunity, he'd volunteer to help. When a call was patched through to the Shark Tank, he'd hop off his call and head over with an abundance of suggestions. He wanted a promotion and he felt it was coming soon. There was a tension between wanting a terrible caller and dreading the insults that kept some call center employees awake at night. Ben's hand had been up and Jessica jumped on his call, listening for abusive behavior.

"What do you mean I can't have MY money?" the caller blurted out. "It's mine."

"That's right, sir, it is technically yours," Ben responded before being cut off.

"TECHNICALLY! What the fuck does that mean? It's my damn money. I earned it. I saved it. Now, I want it!" The caller was furious.

"You're right, sir, but there are restrictions on 401(k) withdrawals. You should have been told this when you signed up. If you take the money out before your retirement, you are penalized . . ."

"What it sounds like is you won't give me my money!"

"No, sir, we can give you your money, but it won't be the full balance you see in the statement, because of the penalties."

"So, you aren't going to give me my money, and that's somehow, in your little dick brain way, okay? How's that not stealing? Am I getting this about right? You keep my money and I do nothing about it!"

"Little dick brain" should have been enough to get Jessica to call over a hall monitor, but she was just sitting there. Ben was glaring at her from five seats over. He hopped on messenger and sent out a group message to the floor: *just got called "little dick brain" over here, normal day at the office! haha, lol.* The message would be read by most, though many people used the internal messenger so in seconds it would be pushed off the screen. He hoped a hall monitor would see it but knew in seconds that no one important had. Ben was frustrated, not by the caller but by Jessica's lack of acknowledgement.

> **He DMed Jessica:** "Hey, you hear this?"
> **She responded:** "Yup, you're doing great."
> **Ben:** "Think maybe it's time to call over the big guns?"
> **Jessica:** "Haha! I think you got this."

It wasn't Jessica's first rodeo, she knew what she was doing, and she knew this caller was rude, but it hadn't gotten to the point where she felt it warranted others' involvement. The captains were also in training and the skill set they needed to demonstrate was knowing when to intervene and when to let someone learn on their own. You never wanted the call to go off the rails in a way that alienated the caller, but you did need reps to make mistakes so they could learn how to be better. Jessica thought Ben was awesome. He was definitely one of her favorites on the line, but he was a little cocky and she wished he'd cool it a bit. The best reps were cool, calm, and loved the conflict. You didn't call over the hall monitor when someone was flaying, you called when someone was shining. Ben was good, really good, but it annoyed her that he was always demanding the spotlight.

Ben explained to the caller that there were exceptions to the restrictions and if he could prove he was using the money to buy a house or to pay off medical bills, then he'd get more back, but that was the best he could do. The caller appreciated his advice but felt seriously misled on the whole deal and hung up unhappy but unlikely to report the call, or worse, report the firm to his employer, so it was a win for Ben, though no one got to hear it.

"Great job on that last call," Jessica said, standing behind Ben's chair. "You really talked that guy off the ledge."

"Thanks, I am glad at least you got to hear it," Ben responded with an attitude.

"Dude, I'm on your team," Jessica said. "You don't need to worry. When you get *that* caller who can't be reasoned with, I will patch you through to the entire world so everyone can hear firsthand your mad skills. But you need to trust me. That wasn't the call that's going to set you apart."

"Yup, I'm sure you know best," Ben said, with more than a hint of sarcasm.

"Later, Ben," Jessica said, heading back to her desk, fully aware of Ben's attitude.

THAT AFTERNOON, BEN was still fuming over Jessica's discretionary decision. He'd worked up a narrative in his mind that she was *never* going to call anyone over. She didn't like him. He didn't know why, but clearly, she didn't want him to be promoted. She wasn't going to let anyone above her know that he was great, that he was worthy of a promotion. Screw her, she wasn't going to limit his career potential. All this time he thought she was nice, maybe a little overwhelmed, but it hadn't occurred to him that she was intentionally ignoring him, until now. This was dangerous because it wasn't accurate and even if it was, what Ben was about to do was way worse than anything Jessica could have imagined he'd do.

"Hi, yes, can you please tell me why I don't see my employer's contribution in my pension account?" the caller asked.

"Well, ma'am, I think that's actually a question for your employer. I don't know what the policy is around matching or employer contributions. All I can tell you is that I see your account and you are correct—I do not see any additional funds that have been added by your employer."

Ben was now so annoyed by the earlier interaction that he was half-assing all his calls. He almost wanted the calls to go badly; maybe that was a better strategy—get the people really worked up, and then call Jessica onto the line. On second thought, he remembered that wouldn't work because all the calls were recorded and surely someone reviewed them. If Ben was caught taunting callers, he'd be fired. But it all felt so unfair; it wasn't every day that you get called a "little dick brain." What a wasted opportunity, he complained to himself.

"Listen up, I don't know if you're still wearing diapers, your voice sounds like your balls haven't dropped yet, so maybe I called the local daycare rather than my financial planner, but if you can get your mommy to come over, I'd love to talk to a grown-up because here's the deal: my employer says they have been contributing to my pension, you say they haven't, that makes me think my money, MY MONEY, is going somewhere, but not where it's supposed to! Nothin's goin' into my account. You with me? So now, can you get your mom, please?"

Ben nearly dropped the phone. What was happening? A lot of callers dial up customer support when they get their first statement and don't see employer-matched funds, but most employers don't match until the employee has been there a certain period of time, usually one to five years. Once the employee is "vested," then they received matched funds up to a certain percentage as a contribution from their employer, as a kind of incentive to stay longer and as a thank-you for staying with the company. Ben had assumed this was the caller's problem, but he'd clearly missed something. He started scrolling through her account. And he raised his hand.

Jessica saw his hand, though based on Ben's earlier performance, she was beginning to wonder if he was going to demand her attention on every call. She intentionally waited about thirty seconds before joining the call. She wanted Ben to remember, she was his boss.

"I'm just reviewing your account here, give me one minute, please," Ben said.

"Listen up, you do not need to review shit, you need to get your boss on the phone. I want to know where my money is going and I'm not in the mood to sit around and babysit you."

"I can certainly get a supervisor, but I think we can figure this out. Hang on. I see here you've been contributing to this account for seven years, is that right? Do you know when you were vested?"

"Yes, that's right. And I was fully vested after three."

"Well, I agree that does seem odd . . ." Ben said as he looked over to Jessica who was signaling that she was disconnecting from the call. He wanted to yell, "Wait, she was so rude earlier, I'm sure she'll be difficult again!" Or "Wait, Jessica! This is a real problem—it looks like she's actually missing money *and* she's pissed! This is a great call."

But Jessica was off. She was now extremely annoyed by this The Ben Who Cried Wolf routine. Ben was demanding too much of her time. He was acting like a real prima donna. There were so many bad calls, and clearly, he didn't have the experience to separate the difficult from the terrible, and worse still, he didn't seem to respect her judgement on the matter either. . . .

"No shit, Sherlock. Something's wrong, and that *something* is my money is missing. This is the seventh time I've called you morons and I'm starting to think you all are running a serious scam. This is bullshit."

"Ma'am, may I ask why you didn't call us when you first realized the money wasn't there, like years ago?" Ben was trying to figure out if she'd ever seen the vested contributions or if they'd never been deposited. But he asked her the wrong question.

"Jesus, Mary, and Joseph, you're dumber than the last guy I spoke with. What, you just graduate from burger flipping school and managed to get yourself a big boy job, answering phones, and you feel important now? You feel like you can dick old ladies like me around? I just told you I've called this bullshit hotline seven times. What are you, deaf and dumb?"

Speechless, Ben pushed for Jessica again, but she was ignoring him. This was it, this was the call that would make him famous. There were so many insults being thrown at him, he didn't know which would become his nickname, but the options were enticing.

"Let me tell you something. You know how you say you record all calls? Well, so do I and I'm sharing this shit show of an investment company with everyone I can. My granddaughter is some sort of YouTube big shot and she's telling me this shit will spread like a cancer. And I think your name was Ben, right? So, Ben, you're 'bout to be famous. A famous fucking idiot."

This was like grandma unleashed. Ben actually wondered if he was on some kind of candid camera. This was too much. He understood she was frustrated, but she was an old lady, a cursing, insulting old lady who had roped her granddaughter into the madness. YouTube? And when she said cancer, he assumed she meant viral. Thank god this was being recorded, because this was the stuff of legends around the office. He buzzed Jessica again. Then pinged her. Then sent this message:

"Jess, you gotta hear this! I've got a live wire and she's going bananas. Seriously."

Jessica responded, "I'll be there in a minute, on another call."

"Listen, I know you're frustrated, I would be too, but from my end I can't see where your money is going. That's past my pay grade. I can see you're not being matched. I can see you've worked there awhile and that the money in the hypothetical match account is significant, so I want to help you get to the bottom of this, but you're going to have to be patient with me, okay?" Ben wanted her to freak out, but he also needed to actually do his job, which was help her and deescalate the situation. It was a bit of a conflict. In the end, if he didn't get the public acknowledgment that this was the worst call, he'd at least get points upon review that he handled it well.

"Right, you understand I'm frustrated. How adorable. You're following a script. I know tactful conflict resolution when I hear it. You're not going to deescalate me, sonny. I'm your worst nightmare."

Ben messengered Jessica, "You've got to tune in, please!!!" He hoped the three exclamation points would convey the point. But Jessica wasn't responding. Stacey a few seats down had also raised her hand, and Jess was on her line.

In a moment of panic, Ben did the unthinkable. He believed in his heart that this was his shot at the Shark Tank and if he didn't act, the opportunity would pass. His only chance at any promotion would be dependent on the luck of another bad caller. And Ben didn't believe in luck.

Ben stood up. Breaking with all codes of conduct, he went over Jessica's head and stood up. In the middle of row sixteen, Ben rose up and, like dominos, row after row of call center employees turned to look at him. Two hall monitors nearby looked at each other, then to Jessica who was sitting with her headset on and her hands covering her wide-open mouth. No one could remember a time when anyone had had the balls to just stand up on his own.

Ben's face was beet red. But he needed everyone to hear this call. He was talking into the headset, but his brain was scanning the room, wondering what would happen next.

"Yes, you might be, ma'am, but I need you to know we're in this together, more than you may realize," he said, his voice starting to shake, "so please give me a chance to figure this out."

Max, cool as a cucumber, felt the shift in energy in his pool. There was a vortex of attention directed at the guy in the seersucker suit standing toward the front of the room. He walked over, slowly, like a lion fixated on his prey.

"Ah," Max thought as walked, "that's gotta be Ben, the Duke grad who's desperate to move up to the sales team. The kid thinks this is how you get promoted. . . . Oh, these self-centered dicks who think they know better."

If this were an actual aircraft carrier, men would die if someone decided he knew better than his superior officer. This was not an aircraft carrier, but that was the metaphor Max liked best and this kind of egregious behavior wouldn't stand.

Jessica was ticked off too. Anyone she made eye contact with got a big eye roll. She'd wondered if he might be too cocky for his own good before, but now she was sure. If he wasn't fired, she'd make sure he was moved off her line. This wasn't cool. She was sure this would somehow reflect poorly on her and her leadership skills. This day sucked and she just wanted it to be over. Why did Ben have to do this? *He'd be canned*, she thought.

"Pop it on the speaker," Max said to one of his hall monitors. "This kid thinks this is his ticket outta here, so let's all take a listen."

As soon as Ben heard his voice booming through the PA, he felt a sense of relief. At last someone acknowledged his judgment was right. He started to gather up his notes to walk to the Shark Tank, but one of the hall monitors held up his hand in a stop gesture. *Stop?* Ben mouthed, unsure what was going on. The hall monitor nodded. "Stay right there," he said. Ben nodded and caught a glance from Jessica who gave him a forced smile that clearly said, "You're a jerk."

"I'm gunna speak real slow as to give you a chance to catch up." Granny's voice sounded even meaner over the loudspeaker. As she spoke, Ben prayed that she'd say the most offensive thing he could imagine, that she'd excoriate him right there for all to hear. Instead she said, "Get your momma and put her on the phone. I do not want to talk to you anymore. This is fucking ridiculous, I have tens of thousands of dollars missing, I don't need your team spirit, I need someone to find my money! GO GET YOUR BOSS!"

There were certain things you learned in the week-long training before you were given a phone line. One of them was, if someone asks to speak to your boss you have one chance to convince them you can handle it. If they ask again, you must get your supervisor. In this case, Grandma had asked twice and if Ben weren't a renegade, he would have gotten Jessica to address the client's calls for a supervisor. But, no one knew—yet—that she'd started the call asking for a supervisor. Now that he was off the rails, how could he turn the call over?

"I think we can work on this. I see here there's a number listed for your HR department. Why don't I give them a call and the three of us can sort through this. . . ."

Grandma then let out what sounded like a howl, only higher pitched. "I feel like you're holding me hostage!" she yelled for all to hear. "This is ridiculous—get your fucking boss on the phone or this whole thing spreads like cancer. NOW!"

Before Ben could say another word, he heard Jessica's calm voice. "Hello, I am Ben's boss. My name is Jessica. I am so sorry you've been having a hard time with Ben. Let me see if I can help."

She'd hijacked his call. Or maybe saved him. What had happened? Ben was in a state of shock—this had not worked out as planned. He only meant to get the recognition he deserved and now he felt like the idiot Granny claimed he was.

Max was standing behind Ben. "Turn the headset off and come with me."

Ben followed Max down row after row of eyes staring back at him. Everyone was watching. When they got to Max's glass-walled office, the stare penetrated through. But Ben was focused on Max.

"I'm so sorry," Ben started. "I just couldn't get Jess to tune in and I thought it was going to be a call for the Shark Tank. That lady was going nuts, you should read through the transcript."

"You need to take ownership of what happened out there." Max had a lot to say and he was trying to be measured. "What am I supposed to do if every time someone thinks they've got a wild call they just stand up and break all the protocols? What would happen if we had five, ten, fifty people stand up because they decided they needed the attention? What would happen to our floor?"

"Yeah, I see what you're saying, it would be chaos. I get it," Ben said.

"But you actually don't seem to get it," Max said.

"Well, I tried to get Jess on the line. I tried but she was, well, she was ignoring me."

"She was ignoring you? So, it's her fault you stood up?"

"Well, it's not her fault, but that was why I did it."

"You really don't seem to get the ownership stuff, do you?" Max was getting mad. "Listen, Ben, I know you're smart and you have big plans for yourself, but first you need to learn the rules. If you break the rules, it had better be because the building is on fire, not because your five minutes of fame is passing by. Ask anyone who's graduated from the pool and they'll tell you they had dozens of outrageous calls before they were ever invited into the Shark Tank. Those calls informed them, taught them, instructed them on how to handle it when they were finally in the spotlight. They did not throw the systems in the garbage nor did they throw their bosses under the table. Your behavior today makes me think any kind of promotion is a long way off. Long way. That's all."

> ∨ *If you break the rules, it had better be because the*
> ∨ *building is on fire, not because your five minutes of*
> ∨ *fame is passing by.*

Ben left the room wondering how he'd started the day thinking a promotion was imminent and now felt like he was scraping the bottom of the pool. He knew the chain of command was important, but he hadn't recognized how much his desire for attention and recognition had cost him. It would take him two more years before he was called into the Shark Tank and another year to be promoted out of the pool.

Years later, Jessica and Ben were again on the same team. His mistake was legendary and the two had learned to laugh about those early days. Jessica had told Ben she had in fact recommended him for a promotion before he stood up before 1,600 people and got his ass handed to him by an angry grandma, and that he'd blown it with his stunt.

Ben, upon reflection, realized he probably needed that setback. He was capable, and he was good at handling clients, but he hadn't fully appreciated his superiors' abilities in relation to his role. After that, he did. It was a hard lesson, but one he says taught him a lot about his own shortcomings and insecurity and need for validation, all of which cost him a promotion back in the day.

Key Takeaways

- Remember your place within the organization.
- Before you break a rule or break rank, consider the serious consequences.
- Most of your career trajectory will depend on you building relationships with people you work with; do not usurp another person's authority lightly.
- Sometimes there are reasons for protocols that you are not privy to; try to respect the order. It may be there for good a reason.

SIX

No Need for a Strategy, Everything Happens in Good Time

Anyone who doesn't have a road map to their dream job is unlikely to land it. The caveat to that advice is that all plans must be flexible in design. Most successful people will tell you their path to the top was not one they could have planned. So why bother with strategy? Well, simply put, without a map you'll be lost. With a plan, you can easily identify opportunities, some of which won't have presented themselves to you at the time of making the actual plan. If you are hiking in the woods without a map, you might have a great time, and you might also get lost. Having a map allows you to chart your course, but it doesn't bind you to that course; instead it gives you options. The trail forks and your map allows you to make a choice. One way may be faster or safer or more beautiful or more challenging, etc., and with a plan, you get to make that call. Without it, you're aimlessly wandering, which can be nice in the woods, but a waste of time in your career.

Having a strategy can be as detailed or as loose as you choose. When you're just starting out, you need to be open-minded and aware that your goals and interests can change in short order. Instead of planning specific steps or specific roles at specific companies, try setting growth goals for yourself. Think of the skills you'll need to get the best jobs in the future. What are some personal habits or traits you should ditch in the first five years out of college? What are common traits you see in leaders you respect? How can you adopt them and make them your own? What are some pitfalls you stumble into? Excuses you make? You don't have to tell anyone, but make a list for yourself. Then write down when you tend to make those excuses and why. Are they ever legit? Are they a way of handling pressure, deadlines, commitments? How can you work on those? What would be a strategy to prevent ever having to use one of those excuses again?

Try this quiz:

WHEN YOU CALL IN SICK, BUT YOU'RE NOT, WHAT'S USUALLY HAPPENING AROUND YOU?

A. You're hungover.

B. You're scared to present at a big meeting.

C. You're bored at work and super into a Netflix marathon.

D. You're feeling anxious around your coworkers.
They all seem to be friends, and no one invites you out.

E. All of the above.

What do all of those answers have in common?

What does your answer say about your priorities?

When else do you avoid hard encounters in your life?

What would be a better way to handle this, so you don't get yourself stuck in a cycle of calling out when you don't feel up to going in? If you can't face the hard stuff, you're less likely to be viewed as a candidate for a promotion.

Here's an example of how you can "handle" these issues:

A. You're hungover.

DON'T DRINK SO MUCH or force yourself to go to work as punishment for overindulging. You'll be miserable and maybe you'll learn your coworkers don't enjoy your after-party stink.

B. You're scared to make a presentation at a big meeting.

The best way to get over this fear is just to do it, do it, do it. Volunteer for every presentation you can. You'll hate every minute until you realize you can do it in your sleep, and you'll move on to something else you hate doing.

C. You're bored at work and super into a Netflix marathon. It's hard to get up, dressed, and into the office every day.

Find something at work that stimulates you or get a new job. You will spend the majority of your life at work. It is important to find a job that gives you a sense of purpose. Once you do, you'll be compelled to go, because you'll be working toward something bigger than yourself. That sense of contribution will make you work harder, because the duties will be about more than getting paid; the experience will become a part of your identity. Even finding friends at work can help pull you off the couch. While a sense of purpose is the goal, spending time with people you like is a great first step. Recent grads often find it hard to connect when they first enter the workforce, because they're used to being in school with peers their age. Soon enough, you'll find your cohort at the office and things will click either socially or because of a shared mission around the work. We all love a great Netflix marathon, but save those for the weekends.

D. You're feeling anxious around your coworkers.
They all seem to be friends, and no one invites you out.

The best way to be invited to something is to express an interest. "Oh, you all go to Emily's for happy hour? I love that place, maybe I'll see you there." Don't stand on the sidelines, get in the game. Most offices have politics, but that's not to say you should assume you're not invited. It may be they don't want to cross a boundary with you, but if you showed you wanted to hang, they'd be happy to have you. You can also always offer to help someone with their work as a way of developing a friendship in a non-creepy way. You can ask what they're working on and express an interest in that project. Offer to help with remedial tasks and the person will likely think you're kind and generous and soon offer to return the favor. When people help others, they are almost always promoted in that person's eyes.

Having a strategy for any problem is helpful. Here's one strategy that might allow you to plan out your career trajectory: Your first job out of college should be all about learning to work.

You've had summer jobs, internships, and so forth, but when you're out in the real world you realize there are good days and bad days. But the bad days feel less painful if you're around people you respect, in an industry that stimulates you, and the goal with that first job is to learn at least a few skills that will help you get your next job. The biggest accomplishment you should aim for in this first position is a glowing recommendation from your first real boss. That will allow you to move on in a powerful way. It will show you worked hard, did a good job, and that you're ready for the next move.

That great recommendation will show your new boss you're up for the challenge, whether it is getting her coffee or brainstorming her next big project with her. You need to do the grunt work in the first gig to get the next level position with the great boss at job number two. The second job should be all about your boss. Find someone to work for that you respect and want to emulate, rather than finding a specific job. Linking up with someone in a field that you are interested in will help you immeasurably down the road.

From there you'll have options. Even if job one and two weren't in the same industry, you've proven you can work hard and you've likely acquired some useful skills. You're now a good candidate for grad school; you are armed with glowing recommendations and real-world experiences. Now, you can start thinking about becoming captain of your own ship in a more methodical way. You know what excites you, what type of worker you are, where you thrive and where you drag. That self-awareness will serve you well for the rest of your career. You need to start strong. If you didn't have this strategy before, it is never too late to implement it. Especially for those interested in switching careers, it's always an option to offer to take an entry-level grunt gig, and think of it as a chance to learn the business without assuming the risks; something entrepreneurs benefit from immensely.

∨ *Having a strategy for any problem is helpful. Here's*
∨ *one strategy that might allow you to plan out your*
∨ *career trajectory: Your first job out of college should*
∨ *be all about learning to work.*

SEVEN

Find a Mentor and Do Everything He or She Suggests

C arl Jung had Sigmund Freud; Yves Saint-Laurent had Christian Dior; Mark Zuckerberg had Steve Jobs; even Pope Benedict XVI says he was mentored by Pope John Paul II. It can feel like finding your mentor is almost as important as finding your job! But, beware, a mentor can also cramp your style, and sometimes taking a mentor's advice whole cloth will prevent you from nabbing that promotion. You want to take advice, but always be true to who you are.

When Charlotte started in her junior analyst role in the private wealth management division of the best investment bank in the world, she was full of gusto. Her ability to preempt high-maintenance clients' needs was a winning strategy.

Outlook was booked with reminders of graduations, birthdays, anniversaries, and even milestones she'd heard clients mention in passing. Attention to detail was one of Charlotte's strongest skills.

⌄   *But, beware, a mentor can also cramp your style, and*
⌄   *sometimes taking a mentor's advice whole cloth will*
⌄   *prevent you from nabbing that promotion. You want*
⌄   *to take advice, but always be true to who you are.*

"In April we're headed to India. I've always wanted to go and cannot wait to see the Taj Mahal," Peter Swanson, a high-profile client, mentioned while Charlotte's boss's boss paid the check for their lunch.

"Alright, always great seeing you. Charlotte will send you the updates to the portfolio as soon as we're back in the office," said Max, VP of investments for the firm and Charlotte's boss a few steps up the ladder.

"I'll get right on it," Charlotte concurred. "Have a great trip to India if I don't see you before then."

The group stood and dressed in coats, hats, scarves, and gloves preparing to confront the freezing January wind tunnels created by the walls of skyscrapers that defined midtown Manhattan. India sounded delightfully opposite of Charlotte's brutal winter walk back to the office.

As soon as she got back to her desk, she fired off the client's revised portfolio plan, which was the reason for the lunch. The firm had had a rough year and was making changes to their holdings, but clients hated changes as it was a reminder that there was a need for a correction; that reminder made them question the firm. Because of this cognitive chain reaction, the firm was wining and dining its clients, ensuring them that there was no problem, that the course correction was about maximizing their potential rather than safeguarding their stash—an important distinction to make.

The bitterly cold walk back had Charlotte longing for the hot sticky air in India. She started googling; she came upon an incredible write-up about the optical illusions at the Taj Mahal. There was a mathematician who explained that these design elements were a near perfect example of how perspective can be manipulated if you get your math right. Charlotte immediately called up the firm's research department—which had a reputation for employing former NSA analysts capable of pulling data on anyone, anywhere.

"Hey, can you all help me find this mathematician in India?" Charlotte said, forwarding them the link to the story she'd just finished. "I'd like to see if I can get her to give one of our top clients a private tour of the Taj Mahal."

This kind of stuff was second nature for Charlotte. She was resourceful, considerate, and enterprising. Those are the hallmarks of top-notch private wealth managers. They know their clients, they know what they like, and they take care of them in all aspects of their lives. But there are some in the finance industry who believe all the clients really care about are their returns. There are certainly clients who do not care about the perks that can—if they're interested—come with highly valued firms. But this is again a matter of knowing your client. There is no one size fits all in any customer service gig.

A week or so after Charlotte arranged for the clients to have a private tour of the Taj Mahal with the famed mathematician, she had lunch with her mentor. Katherine was old school. She'd been working in banking for forty years when Charlotte arrived. As the OG of the old boys' finance world, Charlotte was lucky to have her as a mentor. No one could break down how to be a successful woman in this field like Katherine—who'd lived and breathed this business, this firm, this way of life for her whole life.

And that was all true, but what created friction was that Charlotte thought times had changed more than Katherine did. Not wanting to be naïve or sound naïve, Charlotte tended to keep her opinions to herself. After all, everyone agreed she was lucky that Katherine had taken her under her wing. She knew Katherine had sacrificed a lot to be where she was and there was no way Charlotte was going to challenge her on her choices. When it came to matters of having kids or getting married, Charlotte wanted to have both, a great career and a family, but Katherine told her that was unlikely to work out. It certainly hadn't for her.

Charlotte met Katherine at an upscale deli, where the make-your-own salad choices were infinitesimal. Katherine was hard-core carnivore, so her "salad" base consisted of steak, topped with feta and loads of olive oil. Charlotte didn't want to appear weak to the lure of carbs and went with the traditional Caesar, dressing on the side.

"I've been looking forward to this. I've been excited to tell you how I set up this super cool outing for a client," Charlotte said between bites of romaine. "I found this mathematician . . ."

As she talked, she noticed that Katherine's face didn't seem impressed the way she'd hoped.

"Don't you think they'll love it? They were so excited when I called to tell them what we'd been able to put together."

"Are you planning on going to work for the travel department?" Katherine asked.

"No, what do you mean?" Charlotte asked, instantly deflated.

"Well, you're showing you have a real knack for trip planning. I would agree that sounds like a great excursion, but I'm not sure how that helps you prove that you're a financial advisor? See where I'm heading?"

Charlotte saw exactly where she was headed, it was impossible not to—subtlety wasn't one of Katherine's strengths.

"I just thought it would help, given all the turmoil with clients, to show that we listen and help in all aspects of the clients' life, right? Isn't that how we set ourselves apart?" Charlotte wasn't holding back anymore. Mentors were guides, not apostles. Katherine needed to be challenged; maybe she didn't know as much as she thought.

"Yes, which is why we have services that handle all the client needs. All you need to do is call down and tell them to whip something up so you can get back to your job of maximizing the clients' returns."

Charlotte's romaine was wilting under the stress of the conversation. She just wanted to run away. Why was this woman so hard on her? She had basically picked Charlotte as her mentee out of all the new analysts. Why did it feel like she hated her?

She tried to turn the conversation to the recent acquisition the firm had made, hoping that was middle ground they could agree on. But Katherine was always short on time and had hopped up and declared she was needed somewhere, somewhere other than lunch with Charlotte.

"You're expensing this, right?" Katherine said, as she flung her Louis Vuitton Neverfull over her shoulder, which was filled with a laptop and loads of manila folders. Charlotte faked a smile and wondered if Katherine had brought all those files to lunch because she actually thought she might get some work done. What a dinosaur. Charlotte never carried files—they were all on her phone.

"Sure. Thanks for lunch," Charlotte said, immediately questioning why she was thanking Katherine for the hazing session she was going to have to expense *and* justify to the accounting department.

On her walk back to the office, Charlotte grabbed a slice of pizza. *Carbs are great. Anyone who lives without them may be healthier, but by default they're likely mentally unstable*, she thought.

She slumped down in her black, ergonomically correct desk chair and started checking emails. Maybe Katherine was right, maybe she was too client-service oriented and not focused enough on the numbers. It would explain why two years into this job she was still a junior-level employee. Maybe she'd been so helpful she'd prevented her own progress. Katherine was always saying that women needed to be careful they weren't put into supportive roles by default.

Katherine vowed she wouldn't extend herself to clients as much as she had. Maybe that would make the difference. Maybe she'd be taken more seriously if she were all numbers. Her MBA from Harvard should have been enough to prove she had the chops, but in practice most of the guys in the office did lean on her for admin support when none of the admins were around. She couldn't even count how many times she was asked to dial in the conference call numbers or run off some copies. Perhaps this was being too helpful. Katherine would tell her to do her job and separate herself from the admins.

The new mantra was much harder to adhere to than she'd initially thought. She liked helping out. It was expected that she'd be the first to volunteer, and when she didn't, coworkers weren't thrilled.

"Hey, will you help me think of something cool for my client's kid's graduation? He's super into surfing, but I get the sense his dad secretly hates his son's hippy side. I need something they'll both love! Help!"

"Ah, I'd love to but I'm deep in research on the predicted unrest in Hong Kong and how that may impact our China holdings," Charlotte responded with a half-baked smile. She'd love to help her coworker and already had ten ideas for him.

"Totally, okay, well I just always think you have great ideas. I'll just get him a new board, he'll be thrilled, and his dad won't say anything. If something comes to mind, shoot me a message. Please!"

"You got it," Charlotte said, knowing that doing that would break her new promise to herself.

The good news was all this extra time had made her an expert on the Chinese political system and how it impacted financial stability or, in her approximation, unrest.

Six months into this new way of being, she heard there was an opening for a senior analyst. Robert, one of her bosses, was taking over the German office and he'd have to recommend people to replace him. Surely, he'd suggest her. Right?

"Hey, Robert, I'd love to talk about the role, if you think I'm ready."

"Sure, let's set up a time to go through it. Though I have to say we have incredible client management folks vying for this role and they may be better suited, so please don't get your hopes up, but always happy to talk."

What was happening? He was thinking of the client management people over her? That couldn't be right. Charlotte called up Katherine.

"I need some advice," she started. "I want this promotion. I can do the job. I have watched Robert for two years. I know what it takes. But he's already dissuading me."

"Robert's a prick. He may just be messing with you. I agree you're ready. You are one of the firm's best employees and you are always up for the task. Maybe spend some time before you go in to talk with him outlining your strongest qualities that are directly applicable to the role. That will help frame the conversation."

Say what you will about Katherine, there was no denying that she was a tiger. When she wanted something, she found a way to get it. Charlotte felt lucky to have her in her corner. She would be ready to pounce when Robert was least expecting it. No more nice girl. She'd earned this.

The meeting started out well. Charlotte laid out her accomplishments, her knowledge base, how she'd come to be a trusted member of the team that could easily lead with authority. While she was talking, she was feeling confident. She had this.

"Charlotte," Robert started. "I totally agree with all the points you've made. You will be a great leader someday. And your knowledge of market unrest is widely appreciated. But if I can be candid, which I hope you'll take as I intend, which is to say . . ." He was stumbling. "I like you. I have always liked you. But it's like the last few months something in you has changed. You seem to have a chip on your shoulder. You used to be the one we'd all go to bounce ideas off of, to come up with new ideas, and everyone, not just me, has noticed you've kind of turned inward. Before I go on, I just want to make sure everything is okay. It's been pretty out of character for you and I wonder if maybe you're not happy here anymore, or you're not happy in general."

Charlotte was flabbergasted. What was he talking about? She was happy. She wanted this promotion. Maybe she wasn't 100 percent happy—after all, she'd been stuck in the same role for two years—but she had proven herself. Why was he asking her these questions?

"No, I'm happy. I mean as happy as anyone is around here. I am not asking for the promotion because I'm unhappy." As the words came out, she realized she was defending her current position rather than explaining why she deserved a better one. "In the past few months I've tried to really focus on the work. I wanted to prove that I was smart and that I can do the tough stuff. Obviously, the fun stuff is, well, fun. But proving my abilities is what I thought I needed to do to get to the next level."

"Well, not really. We know you're super smart. We know you get the financials. What really set you apart from the pack was your ability to preempt client needs. When you planned that mathematician trip for the Swansons, I mean that was A+ client relationship work. You were on fire. Every time Peter calls this office, he talks about how he's never leaving this firm because of you. But then like someone pulled a plug, you shut down and no one could get your help with anything. That's not leadership, that's selfishness."

"Selfish! What? Seriously?" Charlotte was spiraling. "I had a long talk with my mentor, and she advised me to stop doing all that supportive work," Charlotte said, anger rising in her belly.

"Well, I can see how that might be good advice in that you don't want to be only supportive. But you weren't booking flights, you were coming up with personalized plans, which is exactly what we look for. So, the advice wasn't bad. She's right, women need to know they're not the default secretary. Like it or not, I know that's just sometimes how the cookie crumbles, so you need to stand up and differentiate yourself. But I never saw your attention to clients' needs as admin work; it's a display of high emotional intelligence that most of the guys around here just don't have. You need to know that's a strong skill of yours and use it in conjunction with a deep understanding of financial markets and then, Charlotte, you'll be running this place.

"But here's the thing: if I give you this promotion now, it will be sending the signal to the team that I value book smarts more than people smarts, because you have redefined yourself that way. That's not the right move. I need someone who can come in and creatively handle conflicts with clients and with team members; I need someone who can inspire and drive the team. Yes, I also need someone with high level understanding of our products and services, but that doesn't trump the interpersonal stuff. At this stage, I cannot give you the role. My advice would be to get back to who you naturally are, stop trying to project one side of you. It's the whole package that's remarkable. You are book smart and people smart and there's a lot of opportunity for the rare person who has both of those traits."

"This is tough, because I feel like you know who I am and you know, as you said, I have both qualities, so being passed over feels unfair. You're telling me to be myself, but you're also telling me I'm not good enough yet," Charlotte said, fuming. "How can I be myself if I'm not good enough?"

"Charlotte, I get it. But you're going to figure all this out. You are a leader. You've been hiding out. Stop. Come back and you'll get a promotion in six months, promise. It's just not going to be until you show everyone you're here to help, to contribute as a team, and that you're proud of your ideas and your incredible curiosity, in addition to all the understanding of China and beyond. This sounds so cliché, but seriously, you need to just be you and it will all work out."

Key Takeaways

Mentors: What Are They Good For?

- **Mentors are not:** parents, bosses, career path experts, oracles, or life coaches.
- **Mentors can be:** guides, experienced professionals, people who believe in you, sounding boards.

Don't Forget Who You Are!

- **In order to be successful, you absolutely must know who you are.** What are you good at and what do you stink at? No one is good at everything. Knowing your weaknesses and strengths is the best way to evaluate the opportunities around you.
- **Listen to your instincts.** If you really know who you are, then you know when someone is giving you bad advice; you feel it in your bones. Your inner voice will say:
  - Ah, that doesn't sound like something I'd ever do.

- I actually really don't enjoy that and could try but wouldn't do that long term.
- I think that might work for someone else, but not for me.
- I love doing this. Why would I stop?
- That's my favorite part of the job. I can't give that up.

- **Mentors do not know you as well as you know yourself.** Even the most invested mentor may make suggestions based on data that is irrelevant in your situation.

- **Don't allow yourself to be "offended" or personally hurt by advice someone is giving you.** The offensive advice is often either misplaced because the giver doesn't know the circumstances like you do OR they are trying to tell you something that's hard to hear, but probably still important to listen to. You may wish the tough talk advice was packaged differently, but it is nonetheless important for you to hear and process. Do not let your feelings get in the way of your growth.

- **Always remember that all advice is based on the past. A mentor will guide you based on his or her experiences and awareness.** That all comes with bias, which doesn't necessarily mean it is wrong. You must listen closely and then apply the advice to your specific situation in a way that feels right to you.

- **The value mentors bring is in the relationship,** which means communicating with your mentor about your likes and dislikes, your hopes and dreams and your areas of weakness will make the relationship more informed and therefore more relevant.

- **Remember the mentor has wisdom to share.** You are lucky to have someone volunteering to guide you, so do not disregard their advice. By listening carefully, you will be able to communicate more effectively, and the advice will improve as the mentor better understands you.

Mentoring in Light of #MeToo

- **Much has been made of men feeling fearful to mentor younger women in light of the sexual assault and harassment epidemic.** Here are some rules to live by if you are a man thinking of mentoring a woman:
  - Do not ask her about her love life, unless she volunteers it.
  - Do not touch her other than a handshake, unless she initiates it.
  - Do not discuss your sex life, marriage, or other intimate details.
  - Always be mindful of the power dynamic that is palpable to her: you are her senior, she looks up to you, she wants your respect, so treat her with dignity. It's an honor to have someone look up to you and hold you in esteem. You are in a powerful position; respect that you're not equals and use your power responsibly.

- Two good litmus tests that I think cover the bases are:
  1. If you wouldn't want someone saying it or doing it to your daughter, don't say it or do it to your mentee.
  2. If you wouldn't want someone in prison saying it to *you*, don't say it to someone else.

CHARLOTTE'S BIG MISTAKE in this case was disregarding her expectational consideration because of a comment her mentor made. Had she had a better relationship with her mentor, she could have pushed back harder. "I think my boss really values my attention to details. I enjoy coming up with client-specific ideas. My clients express deep gratitude for my personal gestures. I think it creates loyalty directly to me, which is quite different than when we send off a pair of Yankees tickets. . . ." Her mentor might not have completely agreed, but she certainly would have respected Charlotte's position and maybe even come to learn something new. The best mentor-mentee relationships are ones where the learning happens on both sides. Use your mentor for his or her wisdom and share some of your own along the way and you'll find the advice is better and the relationship is long-lasting.

EIGHT

Gather as Much Data on Your Boss and Coworkers as You Can

The Best Way Not to Get Promoted Is to Act Like a Stalker

Most of us know that the best way to advance in our careers is to build relationships. Whether with clients, coworkers, or bosses, getting along with others is an essential piece of the career puzzle. But there's a balance and being too familiar crosses the line into uncomfortable territory, which may repel the very people you need to work with.

"He was nice," said Tom, James's boss, at the small accounting firm outside of Boston. "But it felt weird that he knew everything about my life."

You can learn a lot about people by searching online and James Feldman thought it was in his best interest to create a profile folder on everyone he worked with. Like an intelligence agent, he had headshots stapled to the top-left inside corner of each manila folder. Inside there were hundreds of printed-out pages of social media posts, blogs, baby and wedding registries, and even the obits for any family member he could connect back to his colleagues.

> ∨ *Whether with clients, coworkers, or bosses, getting*
> ∨ *along with others is an essential piece of the career*
> ∨ *puzzle. But there's a balance and being too familiar*
> ∨ *crosses the line into uncomfortable territory, which*
> ∨ *may repel the very people you need to work with.*

He'd taken so many seminars on the pleasure-pain principle in sales from the virtual sales gods of the internet that he could sell you on anything, or so he thought. The shticky sales taught devotees that if you enticed customers to trust you, and respect you, then you could sell them a pile of shit and they'd thank you for it. The con centered around the need for *relationships*, a YouTube star claimed. But that was ironic because there couldn't be an actual *relationship*, because you were being told to force the dynamic so that you could successfully manipulate your clients into buying something they may or may not need. James missed that nuance, choosing instead to assume this information was gospel when it came to sales.

James was inspired to get to know everyone in "his circle of influence." He needed to know what made them tick, and then and only then could he win them over. Before he knew it, the promotion would be his.

The thing missing from James's bro-sales-relationship tutorials was that the key to building relationships is learning to listen to people. You must let them talk and share while you listen. Ask good questions and then just listen. Instead, James thought data mining was the key.

His coworkers didn't know that he had actual files on them at home, though some probably wouldn't have been surprised. But they knew he knew too much to be cool. "When James asked me about my cousin's baby shower, I was definitely a little taken aback," Sue from marketing said. "He came up to me in the hall on Monday and was all 'Sue, that floral print from Abby's shower was beautiful. Just thought you should know, I noticed.' Yeah, you noticed all right, but the question is why? Sort of creepy if you ask me."

When James was up for a promotion, he took to his research like a homicide detective searching for a body. When the time came to talk about his readiness and his needs, he was prepared. The interview was with Tom, his direct boss who ran the accounting unit that worked with small businesses, and the owner of the company, Brett. They sat in a coffee shop across from the office in West Concord, just to be away from the prying eyes of others.

"Thanks for coming to talk with us, James," Brett started off. "You've been with us for close to six years and we're grateful for your work. You have a terrific attention to detail and that is important to our business clients."

"Thank you," James said. "I take the job seriously and always try to figure out how to maximize our impact. I believe your father once told you, 'You need to do your job and then you need to get the rest of the work done,' and I couldn't agree with him more."

"I'm sorry, did you know my dad?"

"No, not personally."

"What does that mean, 'not personally'?"

"Oh. I never met him or anything, but he's an inspiration to me. I know he'd be so proud of you."

"Okay, well, thanks, that's very kind," Brett said, feeling confused and distracted by this.

"So, James," Tom interjected hoping to get the interview back on track, "you're used to crunching numbers and getting reports done on deadlines, but what do you think it would be like to join our very small sales team? You know, you'd have to wear a number of different hats, including one where you'd be out on your own drumming up new business. How do you see yourself doing in a role like that?"

"I think I'd do very well," James said. "I would apply my same attention to detail mentioned by Brett a minute ago, to the clients. I would make sure we knew everything about them and how to get them to a place of pain, you know all that. I've been studying up on how to be great and I've got this."

"What do you mean by pain?" Brett asked.

"Well, you need to break people down and then build them up to get the sale. I mean, it's the ultimate winning strategy. Bring them to their knees and then slowly make them feel special and they'll be putty in your hands. And I am excellent at research so I can do a little digging and find some nuggets to help push their emotions."

"Right, so we don't really do that. We're just selling tax prep and maybe some bookkeeping services. We don't actually want anyone to get emotional." Brett was nervous.

"Well, I can't really help it if they cry—sometimes that's just where they go. It's all about perspective. I've learned this: if we decided to see the world as a bastion of crap, then that's what we'll see, and if we decide to look at our crap life and see it as beautiful, then you can push the negative to the back of your mind and it gives you something new to focus on. It's hard as hell, believe me, but I'm starting to get this perspective stuff. Like, I wouldn't be here right now with you all if I hadn't read about how I can go from mediocre to fantastic, but look at me now, having a secret rendezvous with the top dogs. See, this is perspective. Seriously. I think our firm needs some new perspective and we'll all be rewarded."

"I'm glad you're feeling positive. That is what you meant, right? I was a little confused." Brett was wondering what was happening in the interview. He was pretty happy with the way things were going at the firm. They didn't need a new perspective; he was just looking to add a sales rep who would help develop more business clients.

"Yeah, this firm is good, but we could be great. Don't you want to be great? In your post a few weeks back, Tom, you made a point that we all go to work and punch the clock, but what else is there? I heard that, I saw you, and I felt you. Let's make work more."

"You wrote that?" Brett now turned to Tom, wondering if he was unhappy with his job.

"I wasn't saying work should be more." Tom was clearly getting angry. "I was thinking about how nice it is to spend time with my kids, how fast they're growing and how I'd love to have more time with them, but they're at school. They wouldn't be home even if I was. None of this is the point. I like my job. I think things *are* great here."

"Well, I'm not so sure. I mean six weeks ago you were also complaining about how tax season corresponds with your kids' vacations, which means you never get to go away with them. Didn't Emma take the girls down to Florida the last few years? You couldn't go. That must have sucked. Though I guess if you have the right perspective, you could say you're lucky you didn't get to go because you're lucky it's tax season, which is when we make most of our money. That would be the positive perspective, yeah, but it still sucks not to be with your family in Florida. I mean there's really no way around that. I wonder how Pete would reframe that? Florida is too hot or something, maybe. Anyway, what were you asking me?"

The interview was so far off the rails that Tom blurted out, "Dude, haven't I asked you to stay off my Facebook page? It's a little weird, that's all. It's just a little weird that you can recite posts I don't even remember writing."

"Sure, I mean, I get it, but you know you could make it private. You know it's public, right?" James said, clearly missing the point, again.

"Yes, but maybe you should just cool it a bit," Tom said.

That was the end of the interview. Later, when Tom and Brett talked, they both agreed that James might be great at new business sales. His attention to detail was incredible, his memory was top notch, and he clearly knew how to research people. But when it came to pulling the trigger, both men felt uncomfortable.

"He's kind of a wild card," Tom said to Brett. "What do you think?"

"I don't know," Brett said. "On the one hand, he might be the best sales rep we've ever had; on the other, I can't say I'd be surprised if he got arrested for stalking someone or freaking a client out. He doesn't seem to know when to stop."

"I know," Tom said. "I think he's funny, maybe a little annoying and can verge on creepy, but he might be great; it's not without a risk though, that's for sure."

"I'm also a bit concerned about his self-taught sales protocols, how he was going on and on about pain and pleasure, like a pimp or something. That's not really our way and would likely rub some people the wrong way. We could lose clients over that kind of manipulative sales. We are great at what we do, I'm proud of our work, we just need to let more people know about us. I think all things considered, he's too much of a risk at this stage. All I need is people in our small community crying or feeling like they asked for a quote from us and ended up with a private eye on their tail. Let's let him know it's not going to work out, but it's a possibility in the future if he can cool it on the dossier building routine."

Key Takeaways

Forget the recon, research relevant information

- **If you're up for a promotion, it might be helpful to look up your future boss,** the hiring manager, and anyone else who may be influential in the process but do so carefully and respectfully.
- **If you find personal information about a boss or coworker, do not put it on blast.**
- **When you're trying to educate yourself or acquire skills that you think will help you get a promotion, ask for recommendations.** Do not turn to the internet for "how to sell" or "how to get ahead." Sure, there is great work out there, but there's also toxic stuff and you want to make sure you're ascribing to the right material for your goals. Ask the hiring manager or the boss what outlets he respects, or places he's done training. Try to align your training with the company's mission and goals. A misalignment may work against you.
- **Read the room.** Do not overshare, tell the boss that the company is good, but not great, humiliate your boss in front of others, and so forth. These all seem logical, but they happen all the time and prevent people from working ahead. Remember, you could be the most qualified candidate, but if you don't seem to have interpersonal skills, no one will want to work with you.
- **You don't want to look creepy.** Even if you have deep-research on someone, be very careful who you

share it with. Many people will find this violates their personal code of conduct and they'll resent you. Yes, the info is out there, but no, that doesn't mean you should discuss it at work.

- **If you focus your research on public info that relates to the job or the career track of the person you're interviewing with, you're probably okay.** Here are safe things to look for and mention in an interview:
  - Awards won
  - Resume details
  - Published articles
  - Press clippings
  - Anything on the company's website

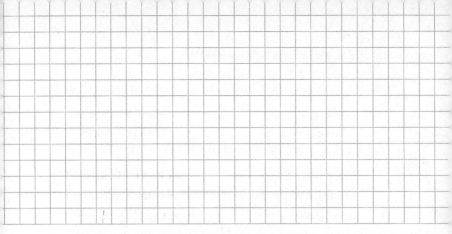

NINE

Be Sure to Tell the CEO When the Printer Is Out of Paper

Yes, it's true: the first week or even month at a new job is exhausting. You go home with a sore face, practically cracking from smiling at each new introduction. Brain cells pulsate with short-term memory anxiety. What was the guy's name that you met by the coffee station? What's the receptionist's name again? Is the lady you met in the parking lot who seemed to know your entire resume somehow your boss? So many new things to learn, it can feel overwhelming.

And asking people their names, again and again, can feel embarrassing. But, remember, they only have to learn one name, you've got to *memory palace* the whole office! We'll cut you some slack on the name front for the first month of working at a new job, but after that you need to master the art of knowing who does what.

∨ *We'll cut you some slack on the name front for the*
∨ *first month of working at a new job, but after that you*
∨ *need to master the art of knowing who does what.*

Jude was a good six months into his job working at a biotech firm. He liked his coworkers, but was pretty isolated from the others. His cube was in a cluster with others in his group; they all seemed nice enough but mostly stuck to their computers. There wasn't much socializing. As with most tech companies, the coders were like gamblers on a hot table. They got up from their chairs as infrequently as possible, usually just to pee. Their desks looked like emancipated teenagers lived there. Half-eaten bags of Doritos, empty cans of Coke, spilled gummy worms, and old stinky socks created a potpourri of smells that acted as a kind of repellent, keeping any sane person away.

The trouble was if you wanted to move up in the firm you had to socially adapt, something coders despised. They'd created a life for themselves where their individuality was embraced whole cloth. They were loved for their intellect, for their stamina, and for their problem solving. But most of all they were feared. People approached them like oracles. They held the answers to serious problems. Unlike other departments, people didn't switch gears or refocus their careers to become coders. You might go from sales to accounting, or accounting to human resources, but you'd never go from sales to coding, never. You were born a coder. But not everyone wanted to die a coder, and therein lay the dilemma.

Because they were so revered, it was hard to imagine giving up the autonomy. You'd have to be a little masochistic to leave a position with such freedom, free from any social pressures, for one with a load of personal responsibility and rules to follow. The only two things that pushed a man over to the *other side* were the money and the status. You could make a lot more money if you were a coder who went into management. After all, you spoke the untranslatable language of computers, which was akin to having a magic wand. But the move came with challenges: you had to know how to talk to people.

Jude was at a party when his friend Charlie got him thinking about a promotion. "You'd be a sweet manager. You're great with people," Charlie said. "Why wouldn't you want to move up?"

"I'm not sure, it's a lot of responsibility," Jude said. "I like getting in, chilling out, and banging out my work."

"Oh, right, and being in charge of the entire server for a major biotech company isn't responsibility? You're thinking about this all wrong. Right now, you have the whole company at your disposal. You could literally take down the whole place with one keystroke. That's a lot of trust and responsibility. Wining and dining people at fancy dinners and flying around the world meeting with prospective clients sounds like a welcomed break to me," Charlie said.

The seed was planted. Monday morning, Jude got to work right on time as he always did. He needed to print out two sheets to show a colleague how he'd gotten a line of code wrong. Over the weekend, Jude enjoyed reviewing the back end of their systems, looking for vulnerabilities and ways to improve their functionality. He often found others' mistakes left sticky fingerprints inside the system.

The printer was jammed. Someone had left it with a piece of paper stuck inside and Jude couldn't get his copy to print. The admin who was usually bubbling around the printer was on a break, but a woman was walking down the hall.

"Hey, I think this printer is out of paper," Jude said, waving her over.

"Hi," she said with a strange smile. "It's been awhile, but let's see if we pull this out what we'll find in here."

She was wearing high heels that looked like they were made from snake's skin or maybe crocodile. Jude couldn't be sure, but he definitely wondered how uncomfortable they were.

"Are your shoes uncomfortable?" he asked.

"No, they're okay," she said, struggling to pull open the printer's paper drawer.

It finally popped open and there it was: his crinkled-up piece of paper.

"Thanks very much," he said.

"My pleasure," she said. "I wasn't sure we still used these things, but now I know we do and they still jam just as I remembered they did." And she walked off with that same strangely knowing smile.

When the admin returned, Jude told him about the paper jam and the nice woman who helped. The admin had no idea who she could be—not an admin from their group—maybe one who was passing through their floor?

A few months later when the time had arrived for Jude's interview with the top brass about his goals to move up, he was nervous. He knew he was a great employee but there were limited positions for people with his technical expertise on the senior staff, and while he'd come to agree with Charlie that he was ready to be promoted, he was anxious. He felt like a fish out of water in the fancy top-floor conference room sans any potato chips or gummy worms.

When Bill, the company's president, arrived he was in a bit of a tizzy. The chairman of the board had to leave town to meet with investors and would be joining them via conference call. While he had studied their backgrounds and knew a lot about their individual areas of interests, Jude hadn't ever met any of them before and it was a nerve-wracking feeling. As he sat waiting, he tried to make small talk, something he knew would be important in the new role. He worried it wasn't going well; he wasn't good at chitchat. Bill stood up and said he was using the bathroom, he'd be right back. He handed Jude a Post-it note with the call-in instructions for patching in the chairman when the time came. "Give this to the girl when she comes," he said. Jude nodded.

Only seconds later, two women walked into the conference room. He recognized one from the earlier incident with the copy machine. He handed her the instructions and advised her to get the chairman on the line for their interview, explaining that he was called away and would join them remotely.

She gave him a telling look, and without saying a word, she smiled and handed the paper to the woman to her right. The other woman then leaned into the center of the table and punched in the phone number.

What was happening? Why wasn't the other lady dialing in?

Bill returned to the room and went right over to the copy machine lady.

"Samantha, I'm so glad you didn't ditch me," Bill said. "Did you hear it's just us for this interview today? John is on the plane. Hopefully we're patching him through."

Oh my god, Jude thought. He'd asked the CEO of his company to fix a paper jam? And then he instructed her to man the conference call. How could he save himself?

He looked at her as soon as Bill had stopped talking. "I'm so sorry, I had no idea. You were so helpful with the copy machine. Oh my, I've really done it, I feel terrible. Of course, you're Samantha Francis, Samantha freaking Francis the CEO! I think maybe I should just head back to my cave, right now . . ."

"What's this all about?" Bill interjected.

"It seems Jude confused me for an assistant," Samantha said.

"Yes, twice!" Jude said, digging himself in a bit deeper.

"Well, now that we all know each other," Bill said, laughing. "Let's get going."

"What are you all discussing?" Doug Stella, the chairman, chimed in from the center of the table.

"Well, our candidate mistook Samantha for his secretary," Bill said.

Then there was a booming belly laugh coming from the phone line.

"She still in the room?" Doug asked.

"Hi, Doug, I'm here," Samantha said. "Not the end of the world, these things happen, and our candidate seems properly mortified, so I think we can all move on."

"Wait, wait, wait, I wanna hear about the first time," Bill said.

"The first time?" Doug said, regaining his breath.

"Yup, Jude here says this was the second time he made this mistake."

"Oh, would you two stop it," Samantha said.

"No, please go on, Mr. Friend, do tell. What happened that first time?"

After Jude retold the story, the chairman came through and said, "Well, it sounds like you've learned an important thing today. Turns out women can run companies and fix copy machines." The laughter whipped up again. Jude was humiliated but felt a little relieved that they were laughing him out of the room rather than screaming at him.

They then started in on the more serious portion of the interview, but even his excellent answers didn't help raise the uncomfortable energy in the oak conference room on the top floor. They asked him a few questions about why he wanted to move into a senior position, but now he just wanted to get back to his chocolate-infested cube and do his work. He wasn't cut out for this; he felt terrible about his mistake and worse that he couldn't find a way to let Samantha know that he really didn't mean to disrespect her. While his move was certainly sexist, it wasn't meant to be harmful, but he'd exposed his own limited view and for that he felt humiliated. The fact that it hadn't occurred to him that the boss could be a woman, or that he was cool hailing any woman over to help with the printer, weighed on him.

After the interview, he learned he did not get the job. He sent each of the executives a personal thank-you note. In his letter to Samantha he wrote:

Dear Ms. Francis,

I want to apologize again for my confusion. I also want to apologize for giving the others reasons to joke about you because of my error. You are an innovative leader and I'm grateful to have a role in this company and work for you. This promotion would have been an exciting new chapter in my career, but I can see now that I wasn't ready for it. My immaturity came through and presented itself to both of us. But now I can work on that and I will. I want to do well by you and this company. I hope you'll come to believe I meant no harm. This experience has shown me that, even though I didn't intend anything spiteful, my lack of sensitivity and awareness was hurtful and disrespectful. Men must work harder to be more conscientious of how our subtle bias plays into our day-to-day treatment of women, starting with me. Thanks again for your time. It was great to meet you again and to finally learn who you are.

Best, Jude Friend

Samantha responded to Jude's email:

Jude, thank you for your thoughtful letter. I appreciate your perspective and your reflection on the matter. It is important not to judge people based on their looks, but mistakes happen, please don't let it cause you any further pause. You are an asset here and we value the work you do. I hope you will continue to apply to more senior positions, I'm sure a promotion is in your future, just as I'm sure if someone asked you to help with the copy machine, you too would help and understand.

Best, Samantha Francis

Key Takeaways

- Mistakes happen, own them.
- Saying sorry is the most professional thing you can do when you mess up; do not let anyone tell you otherwise.
- When we make false assumptions about people, we need to ask ourselves: Why did I conclude that without giving the alternative answer a chance?
- If you're not sure, ask.
- Sometimes correcting a mistake you've made will set you apart from others in a positive way. Taking responsibility and working to correct a problem are two hallmarks of good leaders.

Getting the Offer

The easiest way to increase happiness is to control your use of time. —Daniel Kahneman

The next section will consider how a bad strategy can ruin your chances at a promotion. Not all strategies are created equal, and none are implemented identically, so these examples of strategies gone wrong are important for you to know what not to do.

Once you have the offer, you have a chance to do you own due diligence. Just as the organization has looked carefully at who you are and if you're ready for this promotion, now is your chance to ask those same questions of them and of yourself.

We all have a tendency to focus on our goals so intently that sometimes we forget the bigger picture. A promotion will not be a success if you aren't ready for it, aren't actually interested in the work it will require, or if it will change your life in ways you do not desire—travel, time, relationships, etc.

Once you've received the offer, take some time to carefully consider why it is the right offer, or perhaps why you should not accept the new role. You need to drive your ship. Work is where you will spend most of your life, so plan it carefully and make sure your output has meaning that will carry you through the harder times, because there will be hard times.

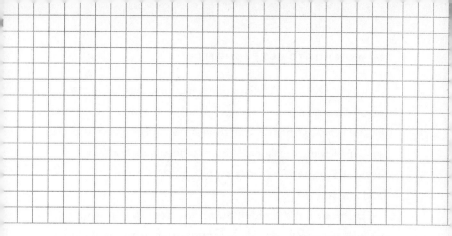

TEN

Always Accept the Promotion

Sometimes the best way to *not* get the promotion you've always dreamed of is to accept any promotion you're offered. When I graduated from Smith College, my goal was to make a lot of money. I landed a job at Fidelity Investments and planned to rake in the cash. If I worked really hard and moved my way up, everything would work out the way I wanted, or so I thought. But that's not what happened.

Once I'd mastered the filing system and the ability to create a spreadsheet, I got a big promotion, which I was thrilled to accept. I was working as a presentation project manager (I especially liked the word "manager" on my business card) in the group charged with putting together presentations for senior managers who sold Fidelity's retirement offerings to big institutional clients. I *felt* like I was on track. Yet, in reality, I was strategically moving further away from my goal. Instead of moving toward sales, client management, or other opportunities with big payouts, I was moving into a supportive role, one with more admin duties.

This is a common pitfall that eager people fall into and one women need to be especially careful to avoid, because there is still a natural tendency for women to fill the supportive, admin roles. Without a strategy, it is natural to feel delighted when you're given a promotion, but it is worth doing some due diligence to answer the question: Does this get me closer to my ultimate goal of that dream job down the road? And keep in mind, moving closer to your ideal position doesn't always mean moving *up*; sometimes it's a lateral move that will give you the skills you need for that dream job.

> ∨ *Without a strategy, it is natural to feel delighted*
> ∨ *when you're given a promotion, but it is worth doing*
> ∨ *some due diligence to answer the question: Does this*
> ∨ *get me closer to my ultimate goal of that dream job*
> ∨ *down the road? And keep in mind, moving closer to*
> ∨ *your ideal position doesn't always mean moving up;*
> ∨ *sometimes it's a lateral move that will give you the*
> ∨ *skills you need for that dream job.*

I was being subtly promoted into roles that weren't ever going to result in me being a big-time player. The skills I acquired, mainly Photoshop, Illustrator, and Quark, would eventually become useful in my next profession as a journalist and entrepreneur, but while I was at Fidelity, they weren't skills required to manage client accounts, which is where the moola was and where I thought I wanted to be. It can be a challenge to turn down an opportunity—especially one that pays well—but having a strategy and a set of questions you can ask yourself and your potential new boss is essential to understanding if the new role is the right move. Without a guide, one is left to the whims of what jobs come up, rather than being thoughtful about what will work best in the long run.

My lack of strategic thinking was increasing my chances of missing out on the promotions I actually needed in order to move into the positions I wanted. Instead of being in charge of my career, I was passively being promoted into dead-end jobs.

I was paid more than any other early-twenties peer I knew, but it didn't take long for me to question how my role was contributing to my long-term goals. And in the process of feeling like my future role was off-track, my goals were also called into question. My ego had been pushing me toward the desire for fancy titles and high salaries, but my true interest has always revolved around people, how they make decisions and how we can help each other. Sales and client management had been appealing because I would be interacting with lots of people and be able to use my natural curiosity about people to help them with their future plans. At the heart of why.

My desire for those senior positions was less about the paycheck and more about the challenge of learning the markets and building the relationships. At the time I didn't have the ability to see this. I had not clearly outlined this distinction and that mistake meant I took the highest-paying positions, assuming they were on a track to the relationship management jobs, which they were not.

I had been naïve about how much of life as a corporate employee is done in silos and my strategy had been to always take the *best* job available to me, which I had defined by salary. I found myself working in an isolated group that had no interactions with clients and only minimal interaction with anyone. That social separation was under-stimulating for me and soon I felt bored and restless.

I was promoted again, this time to a Senior Presentation Project Manager. I was recognized for being good at my job, but that affirmation didn't come with any offers to join the sales team—quite the opposite. I was officially a great *support* person.

I wanted to be giving the presentations I was designing, interacting with the decision makers, and selling the product. My day-to-day was more of a graphic designer position than a mergers-and-acquisitions or new account representative. I would have been better off as a junior, junior private equity admin than a senior presentation project manager, because I would have, at the very least, been in the right department. I wasn't going to get the promotion I wanted because I'd accepted promotions that weren't on the right track.

"Emily, look busy, even if you're not," my boss said when she passed my cubicle at 10:30 a.m. and saw me reading a book.

I'd go into her office and say, "You know, I'm often done with all my work before lunch—is there something else I can work on? Is there some other kind of project I can help with? I'd love to work on something that might get me closer to taking my Series 7...."

Like a scene out of *Office Space*, she'd thank me for offering, congratulate me on being a "go-getter," and send me on my way with no new tasks.

My whole life I'd been trained to work hard, do a good job, be enthusiastic, offer to help, and be open to new opportunities, and if I did those things, then all would work itself out. I was doing all of that and somehow digging myself into a role of a super-duper admin, rather than passing my Series 7. What was happening? I didn't want to be rewarded or congratulated for doing a great job if it didn't lead to new challenges. I wanted to learn how to do the things I needed to do in order to move up into positions with more responsibilities, not to become the top executive's assistant.

Many junior-level employees get sabotaged by their ambitions. You definitely need to work hard, put in time, show you are willing to learn the ropes, and support the heck out of your boss. I was hungry and impatient, and some of that immaturity made my situation worse, I'm sure. However, I was also clearly on the wrong track. It's important to make that distinction. Many people feel they can do their boss's job better than the boss; that is a dangerous narrative to latch onto.

> ⌄ *Many junior-level employees get sabotaged by their*
> ⌄ *ambitions. You definitely need to work hard, put in*
> ⌄ *time, show you are willing to learn the ropes, and*
> ⌄ *support the heck out of your boss. I was hungry*
> ⌄ *and impatient, and some of that immaturity made*
> ⌄ *my situation worse, I'm sure. However, I was also*
> ⌄ *clearly on the wrong track. It's important to make*
> ⌄ *that distinction. Many people feel they can do their*
> ⌄ *boss's job better than the boss; that is a dangerous*
> ⌄ *narrative to latch onto.*

No one knows all that others do, let alone your superiors. Even if you think you're doing most of your boss's work, you're probably not. Calm that ego and look hard at where those feelings are coming from. It may be you don't feel validated for all the good work you're doing. It may be you don't respect your boss. It may be you're frustrated that you haven't been promoted. All of those may be perfectly valid, but you won't solve the problem by degrading your boss in your mind. You need her buy-in to get ahead, so work with her by doing the best work you can for her while also being honest about where you'd like to be in five years.

- ✓ *Calm that ego and look hard at where those feelings*
- ✓ *are coming from. It may be you don't feel validated*
- ✓ *for all the good work you're doing. It may be you*
- ✓ *don't respect your boss. It may be you're frustrated*
- ✓ *that you haven't been promoted. All of those may be*
- ✓ *perfectly valid, but you won't solve the problem by*
- ✓ *degrading your boss in your mind. You need her*
- ✓ *buy-in to get ahead, so work with her by doing the*
- ✓ *best work you can for her while also being honest*
- ✓ *about where you'd like to be in five years.*

In my case, I was stuck. My strategy had been to get a good job at Fidelity, period. I hadn't understood how massive a company it was or how many different career tracks there were. And, wrongly, I had assumed the rest would take care of itself.

Fresh out of college, this was my first *real* job. Internships over the summer had never required a strategy. My goal with my job search had been more about landing at a place with potential, rather than in a job with potential. No one had explained to me that I should talk with my boss or find a mentor who could help me navigate the massive company, help me find positions that would build the necessary skills to get me into the competitive jobs I actually wanted, or find a boss whose recommendation would have helped me move into the right role.

My goal of making lots of money was also shortsighted. In retrospect, it would have been better to have taken a job with the sales team for less money, or even to have kept applying for entry-level sales team jobs until I got one, no matter what it was. But I was excited about making a great starting salary and didn't think much about where that position would lead.

As many say, any goal that comes from a place of greed is usually going to fail. Instead, it's helpful to think about ways you can contribute and make an impact. Those strategies usually lead to success on personal levels that may involve wealth or may not but will surely deliver a better outcome than one that flatly looks for selfish rewards. I was naïve about these important strategic plans when I started out.

> ∨ *As many say, any goal that comes from a place of*
> ∨ *greed is usually going to fail. Instead, it's helpful to*
> ∨ *think about ways you can contribute and make an*
> ∨ *impact. Those strategies usually lead to success on*
> ∨ *personal levels that may involve wealth or may not*
> ∨ *but will surely deliver a better outcome than one that*
> ∨ *flatly looks for selfish rewards. I was naïve about*
> ∨ *these important strategic plans when I started out.*

Fidelity's retirement sector is a place that drives massive impact. The problem was not the company, nor was it my boss, or my coworkers. They all had their own goals and strategies; I was the one flailing about feeling impactless. Had I started with a map of where I was and how that could lead me to where I wanted to go, I would have been better off. But what happened instead was I was promoted onto a track that didn't appeal to me and I found myself disheartened. I couldn't figure out how to hit the restart button while still working at Fidelity. I started to feel trapped and decided to go to grad school. Of course, I wasn't actually trapped and there were loads of great opportunities for me at Fidelity, but I was lost without a strategy.

Key Takeaways

Chart your course

- **Imagine where you'd like to be in five years.** What does the role look like?
- **Write out how you think you might get that role.**
  - Research that role, talk to people who have that position, ask them what their career path was to get there.
  - Think about the options you have in front of you—which is most likely to lead to that five-year position?

Don't say yes to every promotion, take a beat

- **Think of your promotions like a "Choose Your Own Adventure book."** Different options are like doors that open to different roads, and picking which door to walk through matters. Ask yourself:

- Does this new role get me closer to my ideal position?
- Will I acquire skills I do not currently have in this new position?
- Is my potential new boss someone I respect and want to work for?
- Is my potential new boss someone I will learn and grow under?
- Will the reference from my potential new boss help me get the next job I want?
- Have other people with my dream job had this job I'm being offered? Is it a stepping stone?
- Is the team I'll be working with made up of people with complementary skills that I will be able to contribute to? And will those contacts form an important network for me?

- **Most people start out either in a training program or in a supportive role; from there you can go in many different directions.** Ask your boss, who you're supporting, what she thinks you'd be best suited for and why. Tell her why you want that five-year job and ask her what skills you need to be working on to get it.

- **There is no shame in telling everyone what promotions you're hoping to get.** Not that you're expecting to be promoted prematurely, but that you have a plan and you'd love for others to be on your team supporting your dreams.

- **Work hard and know you have options.** Whether at your current company, at a competitor, or going back to school, you have tons of paths you can pick from. You just need to decide your next move. When we feel "stuck" we tend to lose focus so unstick yourself by thinking clearly about your next two moves.

ELEVEN

Forget Your Boss Is a Person with Feelings Too and Threaten to Leave

When it comes to understanding our value, all we have to do is look to primates to decode the power of a counteroffer. Humans and primates tend to want what we don't have, especially if we see someone else has it! But the counteroffer is still a delicate strategy, because you're essentially manipulating those in charge to do what you want: want you more. And moves designed to change someone's desires often backfire, big-time.

One of my favorite behavioral experiments looked at this phenomenon in Capuchin monkeys. Two monkeys are in cages side-by-side. They are each taught to hand the scientists a rock and are then rewarded with a piece of cucumber. The monkeys dutifully perform the task, taking turns as the researcher goes between their cages. They seem to love the cucumbers. Then randomly the facilitator gives one monkey a grape, instead of a slice of cucumber. When she returns to the other monkey and continues to give him cucumber, he gets mad, throws the vegetable out of his cage, and begins pounding on it in protest. The cucumbers are worthless; he only wants grapes now that he's seen his fellow monkey has one. But most social scientists will caution, keep this game up and soon *nothing* will be good enough. Translate those experiments into the human world of promotions and you may find mishandled counteroffers may also backfire into a steaming pile of resentment. When the monkeys become resentful of the game, they refuse to engage at all. Humans tend to respond in similar ways.

The reverse is also true: show your bosses you have no interest in ever leaving the company and they will gladly pass you over as a potential candidate for a promotion. When employees are proven "company men," in that they don't seem inclined to leave, their value tends to go down. The new shiny employee poached from the competitor is seen as a win for the team, but this can be misleading. When someone is a tried-and-true employee, he should be valued for his loyalty.

> ⌄ *Show your bosses you have no interest in ever leaving*
> ⌄ *the company and they will gladly pass you over as a*
> ⌄ *potential candidate for a promotion. When employees*
> ⌄ *are proven "company men," in that they don't seem*
> ⌄ *inclined to leave, their value tends to go down.*

Knowing how the company works is an asset. Yet, most companies like the idea of having top talent and that often translates into looking outside their own business to what others have that they don't. Focusing on promotions, we must consider how staying at the same company may skew your chances of moving up the ladder.

This idea of a counteroffer from a competitor is often the default method of demanding more money and new roles. It reminds the powers that be what you're worth on the open market and may encourage them to fight for you to stay. Counteroffers also objectively show *you* what you're worth. Markets change and sometimes we don't know how much demand there is for our experience and skills. Outside offers provide you with real data about your worth. You can use that information to get a raise or promotion internally or leave your employer for a better opportunity.

In highly competitive industries, it is well-known that loyalty is a virtue, but that becomes complicated by the bureaucratic nature of human resource departments that only authorize incremental raises that are tightly controlled.

Etta was a highly sought-after producer at one of the big three TV networks. She had applied for a senior producer position but knew there were budget cuts across the entire news division, and she might be stuck where she was if she didn't make a compelling argument for the promotion. Her boss's hands were tied; he had no wiggle room in his budget, though he told Etta he agreed she was ready for the role. However, she was advised by a coworker that if one of the other two networks made a formal offer, then her boss could demand the funds to counter and keep her.

At this network, as with most big corporations, Etta and her boss weren't actually doing the negotiating. Her boss said he wanted to keep her and then an internal "negotiator" took over.

That man had a counterpart that represented Etta's interests and the two negotiators were meant to battle it out, keeping Etta's relationship with her boss focused on the work at hand.

Etta understood the strategy and delivered. She was one of the best associate producers in the business; it was not hard to get a counteroffer from another network, one of which she'd worked for before. It felt like a waste of time to go on interviews, schmooze, and feign interest in jobs at other networks only to secure her promotion with her current employer, but she understood it was a game and she'd play if it meant landing the senior producer role.

Keep in mind, Etta was hardly the first to get a competing offer. This strategy had been used dozens of other times, to the point where it seemed like a part of any routine promotion. But something in the air changed during this process. Etta's boss who had always been her champion seemed to be dodging her now. When she asked if everything was alright, she got the cold shoulder.

Ken, her boss, had branded Etta as a defector. Something about a counteroffer from her old network deeply hurt Ken. He felt he'd been played. *Had she come to work for me only to go back to them? Was she really going to leave the team? What if I can't match that offer? I thought we had a relationship!* Ken's mind was spiraling, and Etta's promotion was slipping away.

These questions demoted Etta in Ken's mind. If she was willing to leave, to go back to the competition, then he'd sorely misread her commitment to his team, to their work, to the mission. And if that was the case, well then, he didn't want her anyway. Besides, there was a clause in her contract that clearly stated she could only leave the network during the period of renegotiation. If she thought she could be cavalier with his team, he'd show her.

He'd just drag out the negotiations until it was too late for her to accept another offer.

And that's exactly what he did. By the time this process was over, Ken and Etta hated each other. Their genuine respect at the start of this was gone. What made matters worse was now they really were stuck together. Etta couldn't leave the network because of that clause in her contract, and she had to let the other network know, which surely hurt her chances of ever working for them again. She was stuck in the same role, with only a slight pay bump, but now with a boss she despised.

Communication had completely fallen apart. If only Etta and Ken had been able to talk more directly, this positional bargaining could have been avoided. She didn't want to leave Ken's team and she could have directly told him that. The moment things felt stressed, Etta should have gone into Ken's office, shut the door, and said, "I want to talk about this counteroffer. My understanding is that's the best way to liberate money from a tight budget, but it's incredibly important to me to express my sincere desire to stay here, on your team. You've been a terrific boss. I love the work. Our team is telling meaningful stories and I feel I can contribute in meaningful ways. I would never want any of this negotiation stuff to muddy the waters in our relationship or confuse anyone as to my desires to stay right here. As with any other employee, I think I've proven my worth and I'm hoping to be compensated accordingly, and I hope you can see my perspective. Does all that sound fair?"

That would have preempted any inference that Ken ended up making about her true intent. It also would have allowed them to maintain a healthy working relationship when things fell apart. It might have even inspired Ken to go to bat for Etta more, knowing she was loyal to him. Her honesty and vulnerability could have worked in her favor, galvanizing Ken's support for her promotion. Instead, the silence killed the deal. It is scary for an employer to imagine losing a valuable employee to a competitor. Fear is toxic when it comes to decision-making. Anyone whose goal is to get a promotion or raise by supplying their boss with a counteroffer needs to recognize that they will be inducing some fear into the environment. The best way to manage the fear is to be transparent about your hopes to stay onboard with a new salary. In the spectrum of emotions, resentment lives right next door to fear. People don't like to feel threatened or scared and when they are made to feel that way, they tend to also feel manipulated and resentful. You must manage that carefully.

> ∨ *In the spectrum of emotions, resentment lives right*
> ∨ *next door to fear. People don't like to feel threatened*
> ∨ *or scared and when they are made to feel that way,*
> ∨ *they tend to also feel manipulated and resentful.*
> ∨ *You must manage that carefully.*

Etta didn't last long. Within three months, she quit. There was nothing in her contract that forced her to stay, only the limitations that she could not go to another television station. A massive social media company—the biggest competition to the news business—hired her in a flash. It didn't violate her noncompete so there was nothing her boss could do to stop her.

But this is a devastating story for both parties. Their once incredible relationship was trashed because of the lack of proper communication and an effective strategy that would have allowed them to both get what they wanted: Etta to stay and continue to contribute in a meaningful way.

Key Takeaways

Counteroffers are tricky

- **Make sure you're willing to really play,** meaning you'd actually leave if it came down to it.
- **The competing offer strategy most likely will change your relationship with your boss; make sure you're okay with that.** Even the most senior, professional, experienced boss can feel hurt when he learns you've been out interviewing for other jobs. That's not to say don't do it. It is merely a reminder of the stakes at play. Go forth and demand your worth but do it in a way that can be remedied if need be later on.
- **It is always good to know what you're worth,** even if you don't present the offer to the boss.
- **Going on interviews and making connections is never a bad thing.** You can apply for jobs and see what's out there. Having options gives you the power to make important choices about your future.
- **Always remember that your boss is a human with emotions.** Treat him respectfully.

TWELVE

All Is Fair in Love and War
Do Whatever You Have to at All Costs

S am was loaded at the company Christmas party. He and Finley sat at the bar, overindulging long after their bosses had hailed taxis and headed to bed.

"When I was visiting the Finger Lakes last week, I met with this random vintner who'd been stalking me for a meeting. The guy didn't look like much, but I was below my monthly quota, so I thought, why not?" Sam told Finley. "He'd been on my list for a while, didn't know why, but I thought I'd take him out for dinner and see what his deal was. That's when I learned he's Kip Parker's son. This guy is the son of the vintner of Parker Wines! If I got his account, maybe I could also get the big kahuna!"

Parker Wines' account was the "get" of the year, maybe even the decade. It was a multimillion-dollar deal that would secure Sam's future with his company. Cab Sauv, Merlot, Cab Franc, Sauv Blanc, Pinot Noir, there wasn't a varietal they hadn't perfected. Parker made some of the most coveted wine in the country.

Alcohol is highly regulated and small producers aren't allowed to ship across state lines without a distributor. Wine was a hot market; small producers were popping up all over the country. But, they were without any way of reaching their full market potential if they didn't have a distributor interested in taking on their inventory. The small producers had limited pricing options: if it cost a bespoke winery $20 to produce a bottle of Cabernet Franc, it might be able to sell it directly for $25, but more than that would be risky since most people wouldn't be familiar with the vineyard's brand. Partnering with a large distributor meant instead of making $5 per bottle, the boutique winery made closer to $3, a losing proposition for most vintners.

Those small wineries' best option was partnering with a powerhouse distributor who could demand signage, tastings, and raise the price to $35, allowing both parties to make a profit. And the distributors were hungry; this new market of small American producers opened up massive opportunities for national distributors. They got a cut off each bottle they shipped across state lines.

The antiquated laws were a hangover from Prohibition and about as anti–free market as you can get. All the power lived in the large distributors who had a monopoly on wine in America. This tension between boutique vineyards and large distributors was capitalized on by dealers who acted as matchmakers between the two. That's what Sam and Finley did. They were wine brokers for the elite firm Terroir, whose tagline read: *Climate, Soil, Terrain, Tradition, and Relationships are what makes the perfect wine.* It was known worldwide for connecting small producers with those distributors who could demand higher prices and transport their fermented grapes to wine lovers all over America.

For most small operations, this was their only way of growing beyond the territorial bounds of their state. But a few prized vineyards rebuked this relationship. Parker Wines was one of them. It was run by a retired entrepreneur who despised the old laws that kept the independent businessman from controlling his own destiny, forcing him to work with big distributors who could fix prices and control the sales terms of his hard work. Instead, Kip Parker refused to work with a distributor, which to his credit made his wines even more in demand. Wine snobs would plan their vacations around a visit to Lincoln, Massachusetts, where Parker Vineyards lived. They'd stock up on all the available varietals and illegally mail them home in self-packaged crates meant for shipping priceless artifacts.

It was a stretch but getting the old man to agree to a distribution deal would be a major win for any wine broker in the biz. While Sam stammered on after hours, Finley was getting more and more frustrated. He'd been working on getting the Parker account for more than a year and had zero bites. Was Sam going to steal it right out from under his nose? Sure, he didn't have claims to it, but the thought that it would go to this guy just killed him.

"Parker's son and his wife are super into these YouTube dog shows," Sam continued. "I had to sit at dinner and listen to the two of them talk about these *brilliant* German Shepherds. It was awful."

"Worst part of the job, pretending to be interested in what people are saying," Finley said with a twang of irony, detesting this conversation for many reasons.

Almost immediately after Finley drank his morning coffee the next day, he hopped on the internet and found the son Sam had been talking about. They had a mutual Facebook friend. Finley reached out to his old college buddy Steve, who he had not spoken to in decades and asked him to make the intro over email. He replied to the intro email with his own.

"Hi, Bob, I am a wine broker and I heard last night that your late harvest zin is some of the best around. If you're open to talking, perhaps I could come down and take you out. Perhaps Steve could join us if he's in town!"

Sure enough, Bob responded enthusiastically. Was he being a dick? Yes. He was directly taking Sam's inside info and using it to get the Parker account, but he felt justified; that account was his. He knew it was selfish and undercutting, but it might land him the biggest account of his life, and for that opportunity he was willing to put his morals aside.

Finley didn't really think Bob's late harvest zin was god's gift—after all, he'd never tried it—and as soon as he landed, he took an Uber to a wine shop and picked up a bottle. It wasn't terrible, but it wasn't anywhere close to the perfection of Papa Parker's. He'd been brushing up on the history of German Shepherds and trying to watch YouTube clips of the shows he'd heard about from Sam.

"It's great to meet you," Bob said with a firm handshake. "I think I had dinner not so long ago with your colleague, Sam. He's at the same firm. You all know each other?"

"Sure, Sam's a friend. Great guy. Has a lot to learn, but a super nice guy," Finley said, planting the seed that he was more knowledgeable.

"You all think I'm big enough for a distribution deal? I am a little surprised by that, to tell ya the truth. . . ."

"You know, Bob, I think you've got a great product with lots of potential and for me the fun part of the job is building relationships. I am not a sales guy. I hate sales. I know it's part of the gig, but if I had it my way I'd be training my brilliant Shepherd and sipping wines and making new friends from around the world. So, I'm pretty blessed, because some days I get to do that. And I get the bottom line, so we can talk about all that, but first let's eat."

Bob's order of ribs was in front of him ready to be devoured, but Finley had set off so many alarms he just wanted him to keep talking. First off, he hated it when people repeated his name over and over, as if to prove they hadn't forgotten it. Secondly, whenever someone told him, "you know I'm not a *blank*" he was pretty sure that's exactly what they were. Men who say they're not salesmen are always salesmen. Same with jerks, or people who claim they don't mean to offend you and then say something that's clearly offensive. He knew the drill, but he wasn't falling for it.

"So, you've got a Shepherd?" Bob said, wondering if that was a lie too. "Me too, best dogs. What school of training do you follow? I find the different philosophies to be really interesting."

"Yeah, me too," Finley said. "I've learned a lot from watching the YouTube show 'Forget Lassie, Meet Uma.'"

"You learned to train your dog based on that show?" Bob was even more suspicious, but starting to appreciate the lengths Finley was going in an attempt to bond with him.

By the end of the dinner the two men connected over a shared love of wines, but Bob was still hesitant about Finley's true motivations.

"I'm sure you've linked me to my father, Kip Parker? I always wonder if people are trying to use me to get to him," Bob said, locking eyes with Finley. "I can see why they might think that would work. But, you know, Dad's a tough nut and has his ways."

"Well, I think everyone in the business knows your dad," Finley said. "I would love a chance to talk with him too, but today I'm here about you."

A week after his dinner, he was in the office and Sam approached him. "Did you go down and talk to Bob Parker?"

"Yes, we had a connection and I thought it would be fun to go down and see what all the fuss was about," Finley said, attempting to brush it off.

"You're a dick," Sam said. "I know what you're doing. Seriously sleazebag move."

Sam was no dummy. He knew Finley was going to steal the account. He had thought they were friends.

As Finley pushed Bob for a distribution deal and not-so-subtly asked about Parker Wines, Bob began ghosting Finley, but he did circle back with Sam.

"Hey, it's been a while since your visit. I wanted to ask you about one of your colleagues," Bob said to Sam over the phone.

"Let me guess, it's Finley?"

"Yes, he's been pretty aggressive with me, and honestly, we're not in a position to demand prices that would justify a distribution deal, but he's not really taking no for an answer. I am well aware of why he's so interested in my little operation and, frankly, it's left a pretty bad taste in my mouth. Terroir has an excellent reputation and this garbage seems beneath you all. I didn't know who to complain to, but I felt I should express my frustration. I enjoyed our dinner when you were up here and I appreciate the interest, but please remove my winery from your database of prospects; I am not interested at this time in trusting you all with my business."

"I understand and I apologize, it is not how we like to work, and I understand where your mistrust is coming from," Sam said. "I will pass on the message and we will not contact you again. If things change, please know I'm interested in your wines and would be happy to talk again when you feel ready, or I guess I should say, when you're interested in giving Terroir another chance. Again, my deepest apology for this experience."

Sam hung up and wondered what his next move should be. He hadn't mentioned any of this to his boss for fear of sounding like a spoilsport, but Bob had asked him directly to remove his name from the lists. He knew that he and Finley were both being considered for a promotion and telling his boss what Finley had done would likely look like a petty way of talking smack about him in hopes of landing the promotion. But, deep down, he wanted everyone to know. Finley was a self-centered asshole. He had just ruined the firm's chances at landing the biggest account out there, not to mention that Bob was highly connected in the industry. Gossip flowed like champagne at a wedding when wholesalers, distributors, vintners, and brokers got together. Terroir needed to consider damage control. Before this call, he'd decided the best thing to do was to wait. If the promotion was announced soon, he could let people know afterward and explain he didn't come forward sooner for fear that it would have looked like he had ulterior motives. But, after talking to Bob, he felt he needed to speak up.

Sam told Finley what had happened with Bob. Finley begged him not to say anything. He'd fix it, he promised. He'd learned his mistake. Sam didn't want him to fix it, but he agreed not to do anything until after the promotion was announced.

Finley and Sam's boss, Chloe, called them both into her office. It was time to talk about the promotion.

"Do you know why I've called you both in?" she asked. "As you know, you were both being considered for the senior broker role, but you weren't alone in that pool."

Chloe had a way with suspense. She was smart and savvy and had an incredible reputation for knowing wines better than the winemakers. A couple of sips brought forth dates, locations, and names, sometimes even stories told with her eyes closed as if she could see what she described:

"Oh yes, this is California, but there's something distinctive here, hum," Chloe said, as she swirled another sip around the inside of her mouth. "It suggests the Russian River, maybe Kaplan's Daughter or Bruenner's Hope," naming two prestigious wineries along the river. "Oh, it must be a 2005, when there was the great flood! Yes, these little ones can have wet feet for up to twenty days and triumph," she said about the roots of the vines. "The smaller crop, the stressed-out vines, those harsh conditions, the anxious vintner, all subjected to the unpredictability of nature and yet the ones that survive always make the most delicate and delicious wines," Chloe said, as if she was talking about a war veteran. She concluded it was a Bruenner, and she was of course right.

Her intuition was unmatched when it came to wine, so it shouldn't have been a surprise that those same skills could be applied to people. Sam felt like a kid at the principal's office. He was always intimidated in Chloe's presence. Why had she brought them both into her office?

Finley had assumed he would get the promotion. His numbers were better, and he knew the company liked ambition, which he had in spades. Sam was an honest guy and Finley didn't think he'd tell anyone about the screwup with Parker Wines. In his self-centered way, he told himself that if Sam told anyone, he'd just turn it around on him and explain that Sam screwed up with Parker so he was trying to fix it with the son. Finley wasn't thinking about Chloe's intuition, his nasty behavior, or anything other than the promotion. His internal voice was on repeat: "When is she going to say it, when is she going to tell me the job is mine . . ."

"Often you road warriors think us upper-office types are clueless about the hustle you go through," she said. "I am not. I know it's a grueling job trying to land big accounts, manage egos, and I know time on the road is time away from families and your lives back here. I am grateful for all the work you both have done. And while the promotion is based on your sales record, that's not the only thing that matters to me. Terroir has an incredible reputation, which is well deserved. We only hire the best and we expect everyone to get better once they're here. And building relationships isn't about going in for the kill. Some of our best clients have been in this business for a hundred years. They're not looking for a one-night stand, they're looking for eternal partnerships, for trust and commitment to their missions. One of you gets that and the other doesn't."

Suddenly the room filled with tension.

"Being a team player and always remembering that when you're on the road you are a Terroir ambassador is essential, especially for anyone hoping to move up in this firm. I was at a party over the weekend at Kip Parker's house . . ."

That was it, she knew. The jig was up. She knew. Sam felt his face turn red. Was she going to be angry he hadn't come forward? Was Finley about to be fired? The questions danced in his mind as he wiped his sweaty palms on his pants.

"Finley, what the fuck were you thinking?" Chloe didn't mince words.

"Excuse me?" Finley said, hoping to get a handle on what was happening.

"You tried to steal an account from a partner in hopes of landing a bigger account and in the process got us blackballed from both vineyards."

"Oh, I think there's been a misunderstanding. I went to the Finger Lakes to meet with Bob because it sounded like Sam had a good lead and had failed to seal the deal, so I was trying to clean up his mess. While Bob's vineyard isn't worth much, his dad's the big whale and I wanted to make sure we handled it all well."

"Is that right?" Chloe said. "And how did that go?"

"Well, to tell you the truth, it didn't go so great. By the time I got there, Bob was pretty hostile toward us and didn't seem interested in pursuing much of a—"

Chloe cut him off. "Stop. Stop the bullshit. You messed it up. Not Sam. According to Kip, Bob liked Sam. Bob liked him at least in part because he explained that his vineyard was still too small for a distributor; he liked him because he was honest. Bob kind of knew that already. In fact, he probably knows more about the distribution business than you do; he's grown up in it! You neglected to take any ownership for what may be one of the biggest screwups I've seen in a long time. Not only did you sabotage your coworker, you just tried to blame this on him, and you ran our name through the mud. Where do you get off behaving like this and thinking you're entitled to any kind of a promotion? Not only am I giving Sam the promotion, I'm thinking of firing you."

It wasn't how Sam wanted to be promoted, but he was pleased that Finley got what he deserved. He knew Finley was out for himself, but blaming Sam was going too far.

As soon as the meeting concluded, Finley approached Sam by the watercooler.

"Hey, man," Finley said. "All's fair in love and war and wine deals, right? Friends?" he said as he offered Sam a fist bump.

"Nah, I'll pass," Sam said, walking to call his wife to tell her about his promotion.

IF THERE IS one takeaway from this story, from this book, this is it:

Your future professional life will be at least somewhat based on the relationships you build while working at your current job. Great relationships built on mutual respect will help you in ways you cannot predict. You don't even know who will be the most helpful. It may not be your boss, it may be your assistant who down the road starts a company! Be kind. Be respectful. Be helpful. Work hard and try to find projects that drive impact and meaning in your life. Always remember life is short and your work will make up a large portion of your time, so spend it wisely.

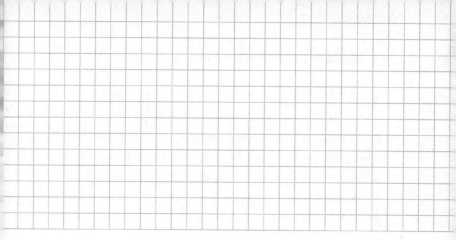

Acknowledgments

I'd like to thank Jill Webb, whom I've known only for a short time but whose impact on me has been massive. Thank you for helping me with so many, many projects, including this one. Thank you for putting up with my inability to say "no" to work and making sure we find time for all of it! But, mostly, thank you for being a go-getter who thinks clearly, who is always supportive, and who accomplishes so much. You are brilliant and charming, a potent combination. I feel grateful and lucky to have you by my side. Thank you.

Thank you to Kevin Anderson, who sat across from me on a packed train from Boston to New York where I couldn't help but eavesdrop on his conversation about hiring writers, which led to a conversation between us about his firm and its needs. Months later when he offered me this assignment, it was a reminder that opportunity lurks everywhere. Sometimes we just need to take off our headphones and talk to strangers on trains in order to find our next book deal. Thank you, Kevin, for thinking of me and giving me this opportunity.

—Emily Kumler